HUMAN CAPITAL FINANCIAL REPORTS

HUMAN CAPITAL FINANCIAL REPORTS

Tim Giehll

SHAMBER ROSE PUBLICATIONS

Copyright ©2011 Tim Giehll

All rights reserved. No part of this publication may be reproduced, stored in a retrieval system, or transmitted, in any form or by any means, electronic, mechanical, photocopying, recording, or otherwise, without the written prior permission of the author.

SHAMBER ROSE PUBLICATIONS
9280 Cornell Circle
Woodbury, MN 55125

www.humancapitalfinancialreports.com

ISBN: 978-0-615-53410-7

"The most common challenge reported by all organizations is lack of appropriate skills within HR to analyze and interpret data."

—Inform Metrics Utilization Research*

"Our job is to innovate, innovate, innovate in everything we are doing."

—Jack Welch, businessman and author, former chairman and CEO, GE (1981–2001)

*www.informimpact.com

Contents

Foreword by Jac Fitz-enz, PhD ix
Introduction xi

1 The Human Capital Supply Chain Link to the
Board Room's Challenge 1

2 The Power of the Contingent Workforce 9

3 Financial Reports—GAAP—>IFRS—>HCFR 21

4 Emerging Perspectives of Regulators 37

5 Birth of Human Capital Financial Reports 47

6 Structure of the Human Capital Financial Reports 55

7 Profit and Loss (P&L) vs. Revenue and Human
Capital Expenses (R&E) 65

8 Balance Sheet: Fixed Assets vs. Variable Human
Inventory (Talent Sheet) 79

9 Cash Flow: How to Get from Here to There
(Talent Flow) 95

10 Financial Ratios: Looking at HR Metrics and
HR Analytics 101

11 C-levels, Investors, Government, and Citizens
Call to Action: An Open Letter 111

Acknowledgments 115
About the Author 117
Index 119

Foreword

HAVING SPENT OVER THIRTY YEARS DEALING WITH human capital strategy and metrics, I find great satisfaction in work such as this book. Tim Giehll knows what is important. He knows what he is talking about and in this book he has laid out a cogent and reliable model for everyone who must manage human capital and maintain a bottom line.

He reinforces the premise from his first book, *Human Capital Supply Chains,* which applies supply chain management to the optimization of the workforce, and cites his research, revealing a widespread lack of knowledge about the growth of the contingent workforce. In case after case he found virtually no one who knew how many temporary and contract workers or consultants were working in their companies. Given that this contingent labor is currently estimated at between 25 and 33 percent and growing strongly, it is a seminal issue that executives can no longer afford to ignore.

This lack of knowledge is a decided competitive disadvantage in any organization. How does one develop a staffing strategy in a vacuum? How does one maintain a competitive pay program in the dark? How does one build a development plan when a significant portion of the workforce is so fluid? This "how to" guide lays out not only the theory and assumptions about the power of supply chain methodology, but also the steps to making it a reality. Even better, Giehll goes on to show the financial rewards for optimizing the total workforce and intertwines the implementation challenges along with his description of talent flow and talent cost management.

This brings us to the heart of the book, Giehll's financial models: Revenue and Human Capital Expense (R&E), Talent Sheet, and Talent Flow charts. Collectively, these lay the foundation for a human capital financial reporting system. Very few top executives know the true status and costs of their fluid workforce, which is similar to not knowing the composition or cost of material inventory. How could one plan a production schedule without knowledge of material availability? As revenue and operating expenses change, management needs to know the state of its most expensive assets, people. Strategy demands knowledge, and *Human Capital Financial Reports* provides the tools for generating and maintaining that critical knowledge.

I turned the pages eagerly looking for what was coming next. You will, too.

Jac Fitz-enz, PhD
Founder, Saratoga Institute
CEO, Human Capital Source

Introduction

IN THE YEARS FOLLOWING THE 2009 PUBLICATION OF the first book in this series, *Human Capital Supply Chains*, I began a small experiment that I carried out whenever I made presentations to groups at professional human resources conferences. The results I obtained were consistent, regardless of the size or nature of the employer represented.

I asked everyone present to raise a hand if they knew how many full-time employees were in their company/organization. Without exception, 100 percent of the attendees knew their totals. My next question was, "Do you know how many part-time workers your organization employs?" About 80 percent of the attendees raised their hands. I continued with the same question about the next three worker groups: temporary employees, contractors, and consultants. *Not a single hand was raised* for any of the last three categories. Without checking first, you may want to ask yourself the same questions about your organization.

WORKER TYPES	NUMBER IN YOUR ORGANIZATION
Full-time Employees	#
Part-time Employees	#
Temporary Workers	#
Contract Workers	#
Consultants	#
Total Number of People in All Five Categories	#

The results of this brief survey demonstrated with clarity that the ongoing focus of employers from a human resources perspective still remains on full-time employees versus the **entire human capital supply chain** (HCSC). If these HR leaders do not know this information, they are certainly not passing along this information to their CEOs—and this is exactly the critical information the C-level executive cannot afford to be clueless about. **Why?** Because the global workforce is changing, evolving, and mutating; and for leaders to engage in meaningful strategic planning in private companies, public institutions, and government bodies, all involved need to have a much better understanding of their (also) evolving workforces.

Information is power and, in the case of the human capital supply chain, workforce information is essential for success. Human capital issues are bubbling to the surface in *every* type of business and in *every* type of organization. Without comprehensive workforce information, issues that have been simmering and developing over a period of years can erupt into financial crises.

The severe economic downturn in the fall of 2008 initiated a "tsunami" of sorts that affected the workforce around the globe, reaching critical mass in the United States during the first quarter of 2009 when hundreds of thousands of workers lost their jobs. Over the next two years, nearly seven million people were laid off from America's companies. With such enormous public staff reductions, corporations lost their credibility with employees, and worker loyalty plummeted. Human resource department budgets were slashed without a reduction in workload, and HR executives continued to be absent from the decision-making board rooms.

As the global financial meltdown gained steam throughout 2009, financial organizations, investors, and regulators from across the globe became more vocal about the absence of 40 to 60 percent[1]

---

1 Mary Weldon, Society of Human Resource Management (SHRM) workgroup report on indices for investors 8.10.10 email.

of the business value detailed in annual reports, 10-Ks, and other investment instruments—the missing ingredient being the representation of the asset value of human capital.

To effectively represent the business value of workforce contributions, a uniform, mutually agreed upon, and respected reporting structure is needed that accurately reflects this important asset value. In addition, the demand for more corporate and government "transparency" from investors, stockholders, and taxpayers rose to deafening levels. From these converging currents of a drastically changing global workforce, a need to better report on the value of that workforce and the growing demand for transparency developed throughout corporate and government reporting. The ideas for *Human Capital Financial Reports* first came together during the fall of 2010 while I was attending a conference in San Diego, "HR Metrics," sponsored by The Conference Board. Throughout this symposium, I was surprised by the huge lack of consistency between companies in how they calculated their HR metrics from cost-per-hire to time-to-hire. Jane Bemis, vice president of HRIS (human resources information system) at the Walt Disney Company, described how most companies are still in their infancy in developing their forward-looking HR analytics, while Dr. Jac Fitz-enz, the "father" of HR metrics and the CEO of Human Capital Source, talked about how critical it was that HR organizations understand how their HR metrics affect their financial P&Ls (profit and loss reports).

"Superior human capital management is an extremely powerful predictor of an organization's ability to outperform its competition," as represented in the 2010 stock investment research of Laurie Bassi and Dan McMurrer[2] (of human capital analytics firm, McBassi & Company) and "human capital management is fast emerging as an essential core competence (possibly *the* essential core competence) for organizations." Their analysis indicates that even the world's leaders in human capital management "are still relatively unskilled

---

2 Laurie Bassi and Dan McMurrer, "Human Capital Management Predicts Stock Prices," June 2010. http://www.mcbassi.com/documents/HCMPredictsStockPrices.pdf (accessed March 2011).

at measuring and optimizing their investments in human capital" primarily because their human resources strategists fail to engage in human capital analytics. HR professionals rely too often on outdated benchmarking strategies and measurement myths. By developing and executing human capital strategies that are "grounded in actionable business intelligence," organizations will be able to "truly reap the benefits of unleashing their employees' full capabilities."

In each of these cases, 1) company leaders who don't know how many contingent workers they have, 2) companies' failure to understand the financial value of human capital, and 3) the McBassi analytics observations, we see an accelerating **"evolution"** in the nature of human capital and the workforce. Evolution is a process that occurs on its own, starting out with spurts of change here and there—and certainly the rise in the contingent workforce and the pressing need for more transparency are both characteristics of a natural evolution. But we are assigning a **"revolution"** tag to this particular progression—along with the human capital financial reporting (HCFR) tools that will accelerate this process in response to the demand for transparencies in current financial and government reporting.

However, the conflict surrounding transparent disclosures is perceived by some as a double-edged sword. When disclosing detailed workforce information to your investors or taxpayers, the same information is being disclosed to your competitors and constituents. This calls for an examination of the forces at work—the conflicting motivations, the key players, the political climate, and the mixture of factors involved—because efforts to make reporting more transparent also threaten to reveal inequalities and potential injustices that may have far-reaching implications.

Inequality in the workforce is "on the rise" in the United States and around the world, according to McBassi & Company, and can be directly attributed to the evolving global economy. Those with money and power have access to even more of each, and technology has made it possible for those on the lower rungs of the income

Introduction   xv

ladder to make their voices heard and organize together to upset the status quo.

Allison Stanger, chair of political science and professor of international politics and economics at Middlebury College, reported that US wartime contracting (in Iraq and Afghanistan) was largely done with a minimum of recordkeeping of any kind, resulting in waste, fraud, and abuse in the billions of dollars.[3] Iraqi and Afghan contractors (hired by the US government) have continued to outnumber the American military and ancillary workers in those war efforts. The contract "workers" are paid three and four times as much as American men and women in uniform are paid for doing the same jobs. The contracted jobs held by workers other than Americans include soldiers, engineers, administrative roles, security positions, development positions, etc. Is it reasonable to wonder how long it will be before the Americans in uniform react to this unfair compensation situation? "Extreme levels of inequality breed social unrest and violence."[4]

For organizations of all kinds, whether companies or countries, certain changes are critical to address inequalities in the workforce that can ultimately result in social, political, and economic disaster. Each entity must start—on a micro- and macroeconomic level— to include as a necessary strategy: **inclusivity** in decision-making, increased levels of **equality of opportunity**, and enhanced **management and development of "human" capital**.[5] These tactics will be essential to create corporate and political stability.

Conducting the necessary research on the human capital supply chain is important in every type of business. The military as well as corporations need to understand the optimal mix of their workforce

---

3 Alison Stanger, *One Nation Under Contract: The Outsourcing of American Power and the Future of Foreign Policy*. Yale University Press, 2009.

4 Laurie Bassi, McBassi & Company March 2011: "The Implications of Rising Inequality." http://mcbassi.com/blog/2011/03/16/the-implications-of-rising-inequality/ (accessed 3.22.11).

5 Ibid.

far more than ever before in order to have a competitive advantage, and for organizational survival in a knowledge economy. The world has changed. The economy has moved dramatically from an industry-based economy to a knowledge-based economy. Transparent access to global knowledge is now reinforced by quick and easy Internet access anywhere in the world. Companies, and countries, must understand and engage their workforces differently than in the past. Analogous to the concept of "just in time" manufacturing supply chains, a corresponding optimization of the human capital supply chain provides a much more efficient method for managing, planning, and understanding the new workforce.

The growing global contingent workforce is the key factor in the human capital revolution. The dialogue during the 2010 conference in San Diego [between myself, Dr. Jac Fitz-enz, Dr. Laurie Bassi, Jeff Higgins (CEO at Human Capital Management Institute), and Jane Bemis] continues to gain momentum within the halls of the US government, on Wall Street, and within associations such as the Society for Human Resource Management (SHRM).

The human capital financial reporting worksheets introduced in this book were developed to bring consistency and clarity to these complicated global workforce and financial issues. Previous efforts to implement standardized human capital metrics across companies in Germany and Japan by government employees connected with SHRM came up against stiff resistance in 2009–2010, especially from the very corporations the changes were intended to help. The stated reasons for their resistance are addressed further in Chapter 5. It's fair to say that corporations in general have never been interested in reporting anything they don't have to reveal, whether it is CEO compensation, conflicts of interest, or unrecorded liabilities.

However, once companies and countries understand that by taking a broader approach, by looking at the entire set of human capital financial reports, the administrative burden is actually simplified. The consistency in reporting will in fact fertilize innovation because information is available globally and executives can shift their primary focus from an obsession with "net profit" to an understanding of human capital "value" that directly affects a company or a country's true financial performance.

Bottom line: Human capital financial reporting is simpler to understand, easier to compare across global entities, and, in the end, reveals previously shrouded information so that it is possible to understand and best utilize the true value of the workforce, which is the core of a company's (or a country's) stability and success. Executives often say that their "people" are their greatest assets—human capital financial reporting provides the mechanism for demonstrating those assets and reinforcing the truth of that exact sentiment.

> **Executives often say that their "people" are their greatest assets—human capital financial reporting provides the mechanism for demonstrating those assets and reinforcing the truth of that exact sentiment.**

1
The Human Capital Supply Chain Link to the Board Room's Challenge

IN *HUMAN CAPITAL SUPPLY CHAINS* (THE FIRST IN A three-part series), we defined the human capital supply chain (HCSC) as the business processes, technology, and organizations responsible for planning, recruiting, hiring, and continually adjusting a company's global "human" capital, referring to all the people (sometimes called "talent") who perform work for an organization. These people include full-time or part-time employees, temporary workers, independent (1099) contractors, and consultants.

Because our workforce requires an ever-increasing focus on what has become a "knowledge economy," C-level leaders have every reason to evolve their strategies from a manufacturing supply chain model to a human capital supply chain model. Essentially, this new focus makes it possible to pay closer attention to the mix, cost, and optimization of a company's human capital. HCSCs link business strategy, business performance, strategic workforce planning, and global staffing for improved corporate financial management and greater business success.

> Human capital (at the level of the individual): "The time, experience, knowledge, and abilities of [people], which can be used in the production process."
> —Martin Husz, *Human Capital, Endogenous Growth, and Government Policy*

In an "industrial economy," **production** meant producing **things**. In the new "knowledge economy," the ability to optimize human capital (**people**) directly correlates to the generation of **revenues**. Only through ongoing investments in an organization's "talent" supply chain will a company's revenue goals ever be achieved. The format of human capital financial reports shows how and where those investments are paying off.

When defining an organization's "talent," the tendency has been to consider the number of years a worker has spent with an employer and/or the number of education degrees and credentials the person may have, but those factors are not sufficient anymore. Some workers assumed that their job was "safe" if they belonged to a particular demographic (age, gender, culture, race, etc.) or if he or she worked as a government employee or belonged to a union. Again, those attributes don't protect us anymore. Some of those factors may still play a part, but their roles as "job protectors" are secondary. In the knowledge economy, **talent** is a combination of **skills, experience, knowledge**, and **ambition**.

The "**skills**" we have usually determine the things we are really good at, and presumably enjoy. Our "**experience**" is a culmination of social, employment, and familial encounters that provide us with context and wisdom. Our "**knowledge**" involves the extent of our grasp of and ability to use the information that is (more and more readily) available all around us. "**Ambition**" represents the "fire in the belly" that drives an individual to continually excel regardless of the situation. These are the four "talent" attributes that employers look for as they rebuild their full-time and contingent workforces in the post era of the Great Recession.

The composition of the US workforce has rapidly changed in recent years along with the evolving needs of the workplace. Instead of a company's workforce consisting primarily of full-time employees, workers can be connected to an organization in any number of ways. As of 2011, one of every three workers in the US was a

The Human Capital Supply Chain Link 3

contingent worker, sometimes referred to as freelancers, part-timers, contractors, consultants, temps, on-call workers, virtual staff, etc. This **contingent workforce** is growing at more than two times the rate of the full-time workforce.[6] Microsoft's workforce after the big layoffs in March 2009 was still 45 percent contingent workers.[7] Contingent workers offer advantages to companies and organizations that result in cost savings, convenience, flexibility, and the opportunity to evaluate skills before making a final hiring decision. Employers can forego the costs and time of the typical human resources responsibilities (payroll, legal, benefits), hire workers on a project basis without a continuing obligation, and have the time to determine if a worker is a fit for a more permanent position.

In addition to the contingent workforce, there is another large group—a **hidden workforce** that includes workers who lost their jobs and may be willing to work, but are no longer looking for jobs. These workers are not counted in the unemployment rate reported by the Department of Labor, but their numbers grew by 30 percent from the start of the recession in 2008 to February 2011. "Adding these workers to the February 2011 jobless rate pushed it up to 13 percent, well above the more commonly cited 9-percent rate. An even broader measure of unemployment, which includes people forced to work part time, pushes it to nearly 16 percent."[8]

These simplistic and traditional "industrial" reporting formulas present a false sense of security, suggesting that economic problems are going away and workforce issues are being resolved. The main drawback with the current government unemployment rating process is the antiquated measurement method—similar to the anti-

---

6 "Why Is The Contingent Workforce Experiencing Such Rapid Growth?" Emergent. com, February 9, 2011. http://emergentdotcom.blogspot.com/2011/02/why-is-contin gent-workforce.htm (accessed February 2011).

7 http://blog.seattletimes.nwsource.com/techtracks/2009/03/03/its_widely_known_ that_microsoft.html (accessed March 2011).

8 Ylan Q. Mui, Washington Post. Bloomberg Business, March 15, 2011. http://www. washingtonpost.com/business/economy/hidden-workforce-challenges-domestic-eco nomic-recovery/2011/03/09/ABHohqZ_story.html (accessed March 2011).

quated generally accepted accounting principles (GAAP) financial statements. GAAP financial statements and the Department of Labor unemployment rate are both misleading for the same reason: they are predicated on the assumption that we are still operating within an industry-based economy instead of what we now know has evolved into a knowledge-based economy.

This archaic unemployment calculation involves calls made to a sample set of households with the question posed as to whether the workers are still working. Those headcounts are then compared to the regular headcount payroll reports from large employers. The messages are mixed—employers are saying they aren't hiring, but the people on the phone are saying they now have a job. We don't know if those jobs are contingent, or with smaller businesses not involved in the reporting, or with workers who are self-employed. In an industry economy (fifty-plus years ago), everyone worked for "companies," so the then-current method of calculations yielded more meaningful results. But the US workforce became far more diverse with the exploding numbers of contingent and self-employed workers. Add to that the expanding hidden workforce and we can see how distorted the official unemployment numbers are. By combining the traditional full-time workforce numbers with the growing contingency workforce and the unreported hidden workforce, we see a much different picture of the true nature of employment

In addition, the current unemployment numbers are reflective of a no-longer-relevant definition of the "workforce." A new calculation is needed that is knowledge based—which means it must be human capital based—and include all contingent workers and self-employed workers that the current federal unemployment calculation has not taken into consideration. The current inaccurate unemployment calculation illustrates our need to reinvent the corporate and government reporting capabilities in order to bring more attention and definition to the aspects of the workforces that are truly driving these organizations.

A disturbing factor related to the workers who are no longer seeking jobs is that the longer they are out of work, the more likely their skills will not match the jobs that eventually become available. In the past this "hidden" group was made up of a much smaller number of students, stay-at-home spouses, and retirees. But the number of people who want a job but aren't looking for one has risen dramatically; and many of these unemployed workers are officially labeled as "discouraged." Odds are that the longer they are out of work, the more likely their skills and knowledge will diminish.

More than two-thirds of the displaced workers who are either unemployed or underemployed are not confident that they will be able to achieve a financially secure retirement, according to a 2011 study by the nonprofit Transamerica Center for Retirement Studies.[9] In the study, 50 percent of the 668 displaced workers surveyed had tapped their savings, and more than a third (36 percent) had less than $10,000 remaining in their household retirement accounts.

These people are part of the overall talent pool that is "in transition." Reengaging these different talent pools in the workforce is a key to bringing about greater economic recovery. True workforce employment numbers must include the entire work pool, including those capable workers who are not employed but could be.

Most governments are not politically incented to identify the real numbers about how much talent is not working. This isn't meant to suggest a conspiracy—it's just that having 16 percent of our workforce not working runs the risk of provoking social unrest. This is especially true when the majority of those not working are between eighteen and thirty years old, vocal, and connected via the Internet. As the growing number of non-working members of the workforce becomes more noticeable, corporations and governments need to embrace more transparent reporting in order to avoid the unintended consequences of this potential social unrest.

---

9 From the Transamerica Center for Retirement Studies, 12th Annual Transamerica Retirement Survey. JobsInLogistics.com June 23, 2011 (accessed June 2011).

In an interview[10] about his book, *The Tipping Point*, Malcolm Gladwell explained that the term "tipping point" in epidemiology is "the name given to that moment in an epidemic when a virus reaches critical mass. It's the boiling point. It's the moment on the graph when the line starts to shoot straight upwards." When that point comes, change occurs quickly. As a result of the worldwide economic conditions—a convergence of technology, social trends, and circumstance—that point has finally arrived where an organization's human capital has become just as important as cash.

In early January 2011, a food cart vendor in Tunisia set himself on fire when police confiscated his fruits and vegetables for selling without a permit.[11] Without a steady job, the university graduate was trying to make a living and support his family. The government took away his only income. The produce vendor had had enough; he'd reached his tipping point or, in his case, more of a "flashpoint." Tunisia had been holding up relatively well compared to other countries in North Africa throughout the global economic crisis, but the food cart vendor's extreme action conveyed his desperation and sparked protests over local unemployment (14 percent in 2010).

The metaphorical "flashpoint" in the United States with the bankruptcy of Lehman Brothers in 2008 and the following global financial crisis in 2009 and 2010 brought about a distinct shift in the role of businesses and their relationship with the American workforce as well as the global workforce. When the massive 2009 layoffs spiked that first quarter in the United States, companies were laying off ten thousand employees at a time. No matter how good an employee, and regardless of seniority, people lost their jobs. Workers who thought they were safe were let go. The message conveyed to workers was: "You're important until we don't need you." Many of those who were suddenly unemployed, just like the food cart vendor in Tunisia,

---

10 Malcolm Gladwell. "What is the tipping point?" www.Gladwell.com 2.4.11 (accessed 2.4.11).

11 Bouazza Ben Bouazza. "Tunisian man sets himself alight," *iolnews*. 1.3.11. http://www.iol.co.za (accessed 2.4.11).

sought out part-time or temporary jobs just to make a living.

The financial crisis initiated a monetary avalanche around the globe, and no country was insulated from the others. The global financial meltdown put every country and everyone in the world at risk, and we could feel how much closer to the edge we really were since the Great Depression in the 1930s. Leaders and workers on all levels could finally see clearly the connection between what was happening in the US economy and what was happening in the world economy. Those connections became more and more obvious from both a financial and human capital point of view.

In light of the slow global economic recovery and the deepening debt crisis around the world, the implications of avoiding transparency are more far-reaching and encompassing than merely adding a few more disclosures at the back of an annual report. As we move from the industrial management of (only) full-time employees to a global knowledge network that uses a fast-growing percentage of contingent workers, now is the time for government regulators and financial institutions to lead the way in developing and supporting human capital financial reporting. By first understanding the principles of the human capital supply chain revolution, and applying them to the development of human capital financial reports, corporations, nonprofits, and governments can move away from the easily manipulated and misleading reporting methods that put the world in such a vulnerable financial position in the first place. Unless we focus on the right things—the workforce that creates the revenues and drives the company—financial instability is a continuing threat.

2 The Power of the Contingent Workforce

AT THE START OF THIS NEW CENTURY, THERE WAS A lot of talk about an emerging global war for the "best" talent. But when the recession hit, that talk quieted down. Employed workers tend to stay put when they are concerned about job security in a tough economy. But as business growth was reported in early 2011[12], the conversation could be heard again—companies were gearing up again to seek out the "best" talent. The unemployment rate finally started to drop a little and, as companies began to grow again, corporations stepping out of their bunkers wondered, "How do we expand now?" As their employees became inspired to take a more entrepreneurial approach to their careers, companies asked, "How do we retain our talent?"

Forty-one percent of employees said that "when the economy gets better," they planned to look for a new job.[13] Recognizing that if they stayed in their current jobs, they might get a 3-percent raise; but if they changed companies, they could get a 5- to 10-percent increase.

---

12   The unemployment rate in January dropped from 9.4 percent to 9.0 percent, according to a Labor Department survey of households. Shobhana Chandra, "US Jobless Rate Falls to 9%; Payrolls Rise by Only 36,000" Feb 4, 2011 Bloomberg (accessed February 3, 2011). The unemployment rate fell to its lowest level since April 2009 in a mixed report that points to a gradually improving market for workers. Jeffrey Sparshott and Luca Dileo, "Economy adds few jobs" *The Wall Street Journal* http://online.wsj.com (accessed February 4, 2011).

13   SI Review, February 2011, 37.

Seeing the writing on the wall, C-level leaders were and still are called upon to take a more strategic approach to the costs and the search for talent as those 41 percent move on, creating a domino effect and leaving open positions to be filled.

In addition, and starting in January of 2011, ten thousand baby boomers turned sixty-five each day, and will continue to do so until 2030. With so many people winding down careers and eventually no longer working, the ground has become increasingly ripe for an understanding of the HCSC in the search for the best talent, which is fast becoming the full-scale global war once predicted. Because the nature and mix of talent as it relates to the economy and education has also changed over time, leaders must rethink their human resource policies and planning practices to better prepare for this human capital "revolution."

Technology and Flexibility Benefits Companies and Workers

The role of human resource leaders has changed significantly. Human resources has ceased to be the overseer of the plethora of transactional activities: payroll processes, benefits enrollments, hiring, firing, employment law issues, and procedures designed to avoid liability. This is the "old school" view of human resources that transaction-oriented boards of directors expected and tolerated for far too long. C-level leaders and boards were content to say, "Human resources takes care of those transactions—the numbers are right and we don't get sued." However, HR software systems and other technologies have made the transactional side of human resources much more automated; companies don't need HR departments to do all those transactional processes. More and more businesses have either totally automated these processes, created self-service portals, or have eliminated the transactional aspects of human resources altogether. Many companies have outsourced their entire HR function—but they have usually kept strategic talent management. As companies move from a transactional existence toward a strategic focus, HR leaders are positioned to join the C-level focus on more strategic goals.

For the workforce, the old stigma of temporary work has evaporated. Changing jobs and moving around no longer means a worker is unreliable or a poor risk.[14] For a multitude of reasons the contingent workforce is expanding and there have been shifts in global culture, worker expectations, demographics (51 percent of workers are female[15]), lifestyle preferences not afforded by full-time work, and Internet technology, which has widened opportunities for self-employment or contract work. The company "loyalty" and long-term employment more typical in the previous century has been replaced with a more universal and flexible work/family mindset.

Contract workers and temporary employees from staffing companies used to be those people who took temporary assignments while looking for "real" permanent positions. This is becoming less the case as more workers prefer the advantages and flexibility offered by temporary, contract, and consulting jobs. Workers can try out alternative careers, exercise choices, and enjoy a self-determined schedule. The average worker expects and has good reasons to choose the variety, control, and flexibility afforded by multiple employment opportunities over a lifetime to meet evolving family, skill, experience, and lifestyle needs and preferences.

According to a February 15, 2011, report from a global staffing firm, Adecco, more than 70 percent of employers use at least one type of contingent worker, and that the contingent workforce will

---

14   The stigma is not really "gone" per January 30, 2011 *StarTribune* article on credit scores not the only thing evaluated re: loans. "Lenders look at a wider range of data (such as how often you switch jobs, phone lines) in determining risk." "…to decide whether you deserve a loan." "Cloud of secrecy surrounds new credit scores," *StarTribune* January 30, 2011) This practice is an example of an industry holding onto "old industrial economy assumptions."

15   Casey Mulligan, "A milestone for working women." *New York Times*, January 14, 2011. www.newyorltimes.com (accessed February 2011).

make up 25 percent of the global workforce by 2012.[16] Projections first presented in the first book of this series, *Human Capital Supply Chains*, suggest that by 2020, corporations and government organizations will find their optimal workforce "balance" with a fifty-fifty mix of full-time employees and contingent employees.

In the first quarter of 2010, another global staffing firm, Manpower Inc., identified a "global talent mismatch" when they surveyed more than thirty-five thousand employers in thirty-six countries and territories to determine the impact of talent shortages on the labor markets.[17] The survey found that 31 percent of employers are experiencing difficulty finding the right talent with the right skill sets for their open positions in many countries and industry sectors despite the large number of candidates. Identifying people with the right skills, in the right place, at the right time is the exact role that the optimization of the human capital supply chains is designed to solve for all types of organizations.

> **Identifying people with the right skills, in the right place, at the right time is the exact role that the optimization of the human capital supply chain is designed to solve for all types of organizations.**

The Arrangement Is of Mutual Benefit To All Involved

Companies used to hire a temporary employee or staffing service, such as Kelly Girl,[18] to fill in for a sick employee. The quality of the worker was often inconsistent and unreliable. Due to the critical need for staff, customers demanded better choices. Staffing firms began

---

16 "Recession Spurred Growth of 'Contingent' Workforce," Rebecca Moore. *Plansponsor*. February 15, 2011. http://www.plansponsor.com/Recession_Spurred_Growth_of_Contingent_Workforce.aspx (accessed March 2011).

17 "A New Era Is Upon Us—The Human Age" The Manpower Group. http://www.manpowergroup.com/humanage/index.html (accessed March 2011).

18 Kelly Girl changed its name to Kelly Services in 1966 for obvious reasons.

doing more to determine the quality of workers so that temporary staff can fully perform on the job. Staffing firms now perform testing, verification of specific skills, and background checks, even drug screenings. Staffing companies also offer online training to make their folks more valuable. As a result of the improved "product," businesses are more and more comfortable with contingent workers.

Another trend making the contingent worker more appealing is that healthcare costs are shifting from the employer to the employee. Companies are having their full-time workers pick up a larger percentage of the healthcare insurance premiums. The cost of prescription drugs used to be picked up 100 percent, but employee co-pays are continually getting higher. Companies are incented to use contingent workers who are responsible for 100 percent of their own healthcare costs. More and more staffing companies are making healthcare plans available to temporary employees (although the employee usually pays the entire premium). Some try to offer more benefits to make their staffing firm more appealing to temporary employees, but most do not pay more than 50 percent of the healthcare premiums.

There is an important benefit in the hiring of US contingent workers who are over sixty-five because many qualify for Medicare, where their health insurance premiums are covered already—making them more appealing and cheaper to employ. Some older workers retire from their full-time jobs and return to their old companies or rejoin the workforce as temps. Some do it for money in order to sustain their previous lifestyle, or perhaps they don't have the savings they'd hoped to have. Some are motivated to work out of boredom or just to stay busy. For these and other reasons, contingent workers are a continuously growing part of the workforce in the United States and globally.

In general, the responsibility for worker training has also shifted from employer to employee, and the incentive for companies to provide training is disappearing. An employer may offer tuition reimbursement, but workers are opting to maintain their flexibility and avoid being tied to a multi-year commitment of employed time in exchange for training or education. As a result, many companies are cancelling their tuition reimbursement programs. Gone are the days when Jack Welch at GE brought in thousands of young managers for training and development. At the time, it made sense to invest in these people when the expectation was for them to stay with the company for decades. Even with shorter commitments, the attraction is diminishing.

Technology has quickly erased numerous barriers for individuals who prefer self-employment or contract work to provide their services. Computers, software business programs, cell phones, iPads, Skype, Twitter, and other technologies have changed the picture of the traditional workplace. With global access to the Internet, the entire world—and all the information in it, is only a few clicks away. Technology has made it possible for physicians to perform surgeries from the next room or from miles away.

On a 2011 episode of the television program, *Grey's Anatomy*[19], an intern used Twitter in the operating room to send out a global request for help solving a problem occurring with a surgery the team was conducting in real time. The chief of surgery was at first upset and wanted the intern to stop the Twitter "distraction" and focus on the operation. But the help offered by the incoming response tweets from all over the world provided information and access to experimental technology that was in close enough proximity to make possible a solution that saved the patient. The gray-haired chief was able to witness and understand the power of global access. Prior to the tweeting, none of the highly trained physicians in the operating room were aware of the potential life-saving solution—but global knowledge was available and accessible. A fictional TV episode? Yes. Possible? Definitely.

---

19 *Grey's Anatomy*. ABC-TV, February 3, 2011.

Alternatives for Workforce Flexibility

Although I have a bias toward the contingent workforce and believe that the use of contingent workers is clearly the way to go, there are alternate views—such as with companies that recognize the need for a more flexible full-time workforce, where it's easier to work with the people they know rather than seeking out others. This addresses the desire on some people's parts for more stable employment, and the potential drawbacks of hiring contingent workers. A 2010 study of US employees (by consulting firm Towers Watson & Co.) found workers ranked "security and stability" as a higher priority than increased pay or the opportunity to develop skills.[20]

Hilton Hotels and Resorts addresses temporary spikes in demand by sending full-time employees from one hotel to another hotel in the region, making efficient use of staff and developing a more agile workforce. According to Jim MacDonald, Hilton's vice president of human resources for the Americas, this approach "allows us to invest more in full-time team members who have a wide range of specialties" and is in keeping with "our ultimate goal to have as many full-time team members as possible."

Wharton School management professor, Peter Cappelli, also supports the view that companies can become more internally flexible (instead of using more contingent workers) through job-sharing, redeployment to different parts of the business, or temporary furloughs.

Some feel that contingent workers don't offer loyalty to the company. A more engaged workforce that is committed to the company and willing to put in extra effort is a benefit. The issue of dedicated full-time staff can have other implications in a healthcare environment wherein contingent nurses, for instance, might work double shifts in more than one facility unbeknownst to either facility, which may not be safe from a patient perspective. Disclosure is

---

20 Ed Frauenheim, "Companies Focus Their Attention on Flexibility." *Workforce Management* Feb 2011. http://www.workforce.com/archive/feature/hr-management/companies-focus-their-attention-flexibility/index.php (accessed February 2011).

important for all involved. Creative solutions continue to emerge in response to the growing need for a more flexible and optimized workforce that is becoming of greater importance to organizations around the world.

New Challenges Emerge

Technology has made it possible for companies to find and employ talent virtually anywhere around the globe. Increasingly, businesses working comfortably with a contingent workforce[21] are saying, "Find us the best talent. We will use them where they are, or we'll move them where they need to be." Contingent staffing grew by 20 percent a year from 2008–10 during the most difficult time in the recession. The makeup of US contingent workforce by the end of 2010 was 10 percent of the total workforce (when adding together temps, part-timers, contractors, and consultants.)[22] Between September 2009 and December 2010, the number of temporary help jobs increased by 495,000 (29 percent.)[23]

The financial advantages of using fewer full-time employees, and hiring more part-time, temporary, contract employees, and consultants, include lower costs, fewer or no development and training costs, flexibility for all parties, and in most cases the contract employee shoulders the cost of healthcare.[24] Companies are using

---

21 Caterpillar Inc. doubled its flexible workforce in 2010, the maker of heavy equipment reported. The Peoria, Ill.-based company added 11,046 people to its flexible workforce in 2010 for a total of 22,066 people. Caterpillar's flexible workforce includes workers from employment agencies as well as part-time and temporary employees. Approximately half of 2010's increase in flexible workers took place in the United States. Caterpillar's full-time workforce rose by 11.4 percent in 2010 to 104,490. The company posted revenue of $42.59 billion in 2010. Staffing Industry Analysts, *Daily News* www.staffingindustry.com (accessed 1.30.11).

22 Staffing Industry Analysts CWS research report, September 2010.

23 Ed Frauenheim, "Companies Focus Their Attention on Flexibility." *Workforce Management* Feb 2011. http://www.workforce.com/archive/feature/hr-management/companies-focus-their-attention-flexibility/index.php (accessed February 2011).

24 According to Mike Stankey, Workday.

more temporary replacements even on the corporate, manufacturing, call center, and global sales levels to cover sick leaves, maternity leaves, and other skill gaps.

CONTINGENT WORKFORCE GLOBAL SPENDING IN 2009
US $ BILLIONS

WORKERS	US	NON-US	GLOBAL
Temporary workers via Staffing Firms	93	381	474
Internal Part-time and Other Temporary Help	89	182	271
Independent Contractors (1099)	243	503	746
Consultants	79	93	172
Total Contingent Worker Spending	504	1,159	1,663

(*Staffing Industry Analysts*[25] and Annual Kennedy Information)

Of the 140 million US workers, part-time workers make up 2 percent (about three million people); temporary employees make up about 2 percent, contract workers make up 4 percent, and consultants are the remaining 2 percent, for a total of 10 percent of the US workforce. A reasonable prediction is that this number will go up by as much as 10 percent each year until it reaches a fifty-fifty equilibrium, when the contingent worker numbers will be in equilibrium with full-time employees. Company executives need to know how to manage a more flexible global workforce going forward wherein 50 percent of all workers are contingent and 50 percent are full-time. A deeper analysis of this evolving management challenge is beyond the intentions of this book.[26]

The US military is also trying to shift from an industrial base (tanks, ships, planes) to a knowledge focus (drones, satellites, rapid response teams). The Navy certainly can't rely solely on the movement of ships that take so long to get anywhere. Consider the technology

---

25 "Annual Contingency Workforce Analysts," *Staffing Industry Analysts*, September 2010. www.staffingindustry.com.

26 The third book in our "trilogy" of human capital concepts, *Human Capital Global Management*, will discuss these challenges.

the military now uses to make war "safer." Cameras on helmets make war zones and hot spots visible and provide immediate information to the central command. Robots are now used to enter danger areas, disarm bombs, and provide video. As a result, modern wars have fewer troop casualties. Company sales people need to have the same flexibility when it comes to better decisions concerning where branch offices are located; they need to be more responsive to customers, and more mobile in terms of access to information onsite, face to face, and remotely with the use of communications technology.

The "Perfect Storm" for Human Capital Supply Chains

As all the different described forces come together—a "perfect storm" has developed that is the convergence of technology, the global economy, the expanding contingent workforce, and the need for high quality talent—C-level leaders have finally begun to understand why a human capital supply chain model is critical for success.

In the 1970s, financial systems were automated and spreadsheets were born. In the 1980s, manufacturing was automated with manufacturing resource planning (MRP) and enterprise resource planning (ERP) systems and new "just in time" (JIT) production processes. In the 1990s, materials supply chain systems were created, giving the end-to-end visibility demand from customers to manufacturers and to suppliers. Sales were automated with customer relationship management (CRM) systems, but many implementations failed due to poor process reengineering and bad user interfaces. In the 2000s, customer interaction was able to be automated using the Internet, and content availability exploded. The 2010s is the decade when human capital supply chains and staffing suppliers are finally able to streamline and automate the flow of all types of workers.

Most people don't consider—or aren't aware—that their human resources software is only set up to track full-time and part-time employees who are actually on the organization's payroll. If an HR or payroll system was installed before 2005, it had to be customized or replaced with a contingent-friendly HR system, such as Workday, from Peoplesoft founder Dave Duffield. In reviewing an HR system, there are five critical features that must be included:

1. Reflection of all full-time, part-time, temporary employees, 1099 contractors, and consultants in the system of record as individual workers.

2. Performance reviews that are completed and recorded for all five categories of worker.

3. Expanded focus on individual skill competencies (which should be verified) and related experience and achievements recorded, not just degrees, titles, and tenure. Internal employees and external candidates need to be treated as equals for new job opportunities.

4. Ability to reflect the movement of workers between the five types, without being removed from the system of record.

5. HR systems of record must be able to handle a fifty-fifty split between full-time employees and global contingent workers.

When Henry Ford built cars, there was no need for a complicated supply chain. All cars were the same. The product parts were all the same, and all the cars were black. As automotives evolved along with other industries, there were more styles and choices; hence, the need for manufacturing supply chains to deal with the added complications. The same dynamic is true concerning the workforce with different types of workers who have diverse skills and experience. To manage all these different types of workers is far too complicated using the old human resources methods—there are too many potential options. An automated human capital supply chain is required to help businesses deal with this new level of complexity.

In order to prevent mass layoffs in the future and optimize our existing workforces, we need to implement a human capital supply chain strategy. Managing human capital must be done as efficiently and scientifically as the managing of other supply chains. This entails translating the best practices from manufacturing and distribution supply chains (from successful companies like Walmart) to human capital, with streamlining, optimizing, and applying integrated technology, just like ERP for manufacturing and CRM for sales.

This new strategic change requires a shift in company focus away from human resources as purveyors of transactions and toward human capital supply chain leaders who are partners in a C-level strategy. Human resources leaders need a seat at the decision-making boardroom table to ensure the success of a company's workforce strategy. The time is right for this shift, now that integrated reporting and measuring mechanisms make it possible to evaluate true workforce costs and make critical financial decisions. The newest investor reports are ready for implementation in the form of human capital financial reporting statements.

3 Financial Statements—GAAP → IFRS → HCFR

Generally Accepted Accounting Principles (GAAP) leave a big GAP

GENERALLY ACCEPTED ACCOUNTING PRINCIPLES (GAAP), adopted more than a century ago and widely embraced by US manufacturing and distribution companies throughout the twentieth century, focused on four key things: cash, inventory, buildings, and equipment. In an industrial economy, the number-one expense is inventory. By the end of the twentieth century, this economic model was being replaced with a "knowledge" economy based more on information and services—with a perspective that has become more and more global by the day. The number-one expense in the new knowledge economy is people—requiring a new set of standard accounting reports and principles to plan for, track, and measure an organization's success and value.

GAAP rules have changed very slowly over the last century. The rules were tweaked and revised over the years, but there were no significant changes from the perspective of a C-level executive. The obvious limitations of the old GAAP, based on an industrial, localized economy, helped bring about a natural change within the global accounting community. A strategic update was required in order to meet the needs of businesses, investors, and regulators who are turning to international financial reporting standards (IFRS). More than a hundred countries already use IFRS, and that number is growing. No country is moving *toward* GAAP.

A Different Set of Rules for This New Paradigm

The worldwide shift in financial auditing and reporting standards was prompted by the same "perfect storm" that occurred in the human resources community. In response to these forces, as well as the confusion produced by the variety of reporting processes used by different countries and regions (the United States, the United Kingdom, Europe, Asia, etc.) the largest international power brokers in the financial world, "the Big Four,"[27] came together and decided new rules were needed for financial reporting that could be applied globally. Those Big Four audit firms, Deloitte Touche Tohmatsu, PricewaterhouseCoopers, Ernst & Young, and KPMG engaged in discussions about how to best develop the new global financial reporting standards. Committees were formed. The initial involvement leaned more toward the European systems, and then brought in the needs of the United States, United Kingdom, Asia, etc. After several decades of discussion, the international financial reporting standards (IFRS) were introduced to the international financial world. At long last, a transformation is set to take place with the implementation of the new IFRS rules.[28] The final decisions for the implementation schedule in the United States are in the hands of the Securities and Exchange Commission (SEC). This is covered in more detail in Chapter 4.

---

27 There used to be a fifth, Arthur Anderson, until 2002 when the company was dissected following the Enron scandal.

28 2015–2018 are the possible staggered adoption dates in the United States. "IFRS Current Situation and Next Steps" http://www.pwc.com/us/en/issues/ifrs-reporting/transition-to-ifrs-status.jhtml (accessed February 2011).

Some of the undeniable advantages of going with IFRS are that the instructions remain brief, simpler, and more transparent, providing a more accurate picture of the health of a company. The IFRS summary document of instructions is only 2,500 pages—a fraction of the 25,000 pages of instructions for GAAP. Similar to many documented procedures, such as the US tax code, there was and still is a compelling need for streamlining and simplification.

This shift to IFRS brings about many other advantages within a global business environment, but nothing is perfect. After more than a century of GAAP rules, we will finally enjoy global financial standards, but we still need to take the next step. The entire process is still a "shell game" of sorts because there is nothing in the new model that recognizes or credits the true value of talent to a corporation. So, overall, the IFRS is not really a game changer.

> **A shift to human capital financial reports combined with the human capital supply chain model is the *true* game changer.**

Although the new global set of standards are more simplified, the IFRS (similar to the old GAAP model) stills uses currency as the common denominator for investments that sees value primarily in the context of "things" (inventory, land, buildings, equipment, stock, cash, etc.) rather than introducing a new focus on people/human capital/talent as part of the overall value of a business. Further change is needed to recognize the growing importance of talent as it relates to the health of these evolving global corporations. The next stage in this evolution uses human capital financial reports that tie in with the human capital supply chain movement. A shift to human capital financial reports combined with the human capital supply chain model is the *true game changer* as depicted in the following chart.

GAAP CHARACTERISTICS	—>	HCFR CHARACTERISTICS
Industrial economy	—>	Knowledge economy
Manufacturing focus	—>	Service focus
Land, buildings, equipment	—>	People/talent
Local market	—>	Global market
Long-term employees (40 yrs)	—>	Short-term, multiple job changes (3–5 yrs)
Primarily full-time employees	—>	Blend: FT, PT, temps, contract, consultants
Healthcare paid by employer	—>	Healthcare paid 50–100 percent by employee
1900 through 1999	—>	2000 into the future

The Danger of Focusing on Short-term Profits

Whether using GAAP or IFRS, both standards still place the primary emphasis on the value of company financial performance in relationship to earnings and stock prices, which perpetuates the focus on short-term gains. But stock prices are not a true long-term gauge of the value of a company. When evaluating the short-term value of a company, it is easier to ask how much cash and profit the company has generated and relate those facts to stock value. The problem is that self-serving CEOs can manipulate cash, profits, and stock prices by simply buying back their shares on the open market. No actual value is generated for investors or stockholders, but all the financial indicators show improvement. Another way to manipulate the short-term cash, profits, or stock price of a firm is to layoff a bunch of talent and watch the next few quarters magically improve. In both cases, the short-term "improvement" wears off in a few quarters when the company does not have the talent to execute its strategies or the cash to invest in its expansions and workforce.

As the recession began to ease, 25 percent[29] of corporations "sitting on these unprecedented levels of cash" were more interested in buying back their stocks from the market rather than in invest-

---

[29] "US companies buy back stock in droves as they hold record levels of cash" *Washington Post*, Jia Lynn Yang. Oct 7, 2010. http://www.washingtonpost.com (accessed Feb 2011).

ing in hiring more people or on job-generating activities essential for economic growth. They hoped to prop the stock prices back up so that shareholders would think things are better, and so that their CEOs could still get their huge bonuses. Companies began to invest in stock price enhancements rather than talent/people.

One of the few human capital requirements for US GAAP-based annual reports and 10-K reporting is the disclosure of CEO and board member compensation. CEO salaries have become exorbitant when compared to the salary of the average worker within that same company. CEO compensation compared to the average production worker over the last forty years illustrates a widening imbalance. Legendary management consultant, Edward Demming (circa 1960s), wrote that this compensation ratio should never be more than twenty to one. If the minimum wage rate had risen at the same rate as CEO pay since 1990, the minimum wage would now be $23.03 instead of $7.25 (2010).

YEAR	CEO TO WORKER PAY RATIO[30]
1970	28 to 1
1982	42 to 1
1990	107 to 1
2003	301 to 1
2007	344 to 1

By contrast, in the United Kingdom, London's FTSE (financial times and stock exchange) executives will not see base pay increases in 2011.[31] In 23 percent of UK companies, executive pay is frozen, and any increases that do occur will be at about 3 percent. This is the third consecutive year that this "restraint" has occurred, wherein any raises are in line with the national average earnings. Other measures

---

30 http://money.cnn.com/2005/08/26/news/economy/ceo_pay/ (accessed March 2011).
31 "UK – Shareholder pressure keeps lid on executive pay" Staffing Industry. 3.30.11. www.staffingindustry.com/media/mediamanager/WE_dailynews/.

were taken to keep executives motivated, such as raising the potential bonus amount. However, one in three companies amended their performance conditions, and 17 percent increased the level of performance required to receive the maximum bonus payout. In addition, 72 percent of FTSE-100 and 58 percent of FTSE-250 companies have deferred bonus plans, and for 65 percent of these, the entire deferral is compulsory.[32] In general, companies and countries are taking steps to better align pay with performance. Aside from executive compensation, which has been a lightning rod for controversy, there are other tectonic shifts taking place worldwide that are reshaping the global workforce.

The concern over CEO compensation and bonuses is ongoing. After the financial bailouts of 2008, Wall Street executives still received their bonuses. It's not entirely fair to blame that on the greed of CEOs[33], because they are simply reacting to board of director incentives that are continually focused on increasing short-term stock prices.

The current focus of financial reports places too much emphasis on profitability and stock price (earnings per share), which only reinforces the ongoing short-term mentality. In a global knowledge-based economy, a shift is drastically needed to put emphasis on understanding the talent demographics (the combination of skills and talents—the right recipe) for what a company needs to grow over the long run. A longer-term approach is needed that puts the value and importance on talent rather than on things (land/buildings/equipment). The need for a long-term focus was only raised again in the years following the financial crisis. Some changes have occurred to help shift that focus, such as the requirement to further disclose CEO and board member compensation, but that is not enough.

Creating a human capital financial report (that is directly connected to the human capital supply chain) will make it possible for companies to implement long-term growth strategies, as well

---

32 Ibid.
33 However, the fictional character in the movie *Wall Street*, Gordon Gecko, who said, "Greed is good," has a large following.

as develop and launch new products and services—the things that require people's imagination and creativity to turn ideas into revenue offerings. The primary emphasis of the human capital financial report is on the long-term health and growth of a business, which is the investment in talent.

> **The primary emphasis of the human capital financial report is on the long-term health and growth of a business, which is the investment in talent.**

The Merger Shell Game: An Example of an Ongoing Short-term Mentality

Most large mergers don't work[34] and don't end up creating more long-term value for investors. Why? A merger is often a short-term solution to a long-term problem. Companies make merger decisions with the primary intent to quickly build up earnings per share.

Consider two companies in a similar business, each making equal earnings. The companies merge to double their revenue. They expect one plus one to be greater than two. With many workers in duplicate jobs, the companies then cut people. On paper, the impression is that earnings have increased (having fewer salaries to pay). The industry and investor mentality was to assume there was a lot of "fat," so why not let go of some people? (as though they didn't matter). As long as earnings per share go up in the short term, things look good to stockholders. This is an example of confusing revenue growth with improved earnings per share without looking at the human capital supply chain implications.

Take a look at the same merged company five to ten years later and we find the promised results (improved profits and earnings per

---

34 Steve Tobak. BNET, the CBS Interactive Business Network. http://www.bnet.com/blog/ceo/most-mergers-fail-so-why-do-them/1619 (accessed February 2011).

share) are still not there. The company is making less money. Those initial improved profits were artificial and short-term in nature. What they got was: one plus one equaled less than two.

The corporate leaders who let go of so much talent realized too late that the ones who were let go were the ones creating revenue by creating, selling, and supporting the products (turns out they did matter). The merger only improved short-term earnings and they lost the talent that would have driven the future revenue and profits. Over time, the results of most mergers were more bad than good because the decisions were not focused on the talent of the organization.

The 2004 merger of Sears and Kmart is "one of the classic examples of two turkeys not making an eagle."[35] Eddie Lampert, who had controlled Kmart, became the chairman of the new Sears Holdings, which has continued to struggle with years of falling sales and ongoing losses. The situation became so bad that *CNBC* senior stocks commentator, Herb Greenberg, described Lampert as 2007's "worst CEO." After a three-year search, a new CEO was appointed in February 2011 and the future remains uncertain. Variations on the merger theme can be studied in the examples of other large failed mergers: Time Warner and AOL, Sprint and Nextel, HP and Compaq, Daimler and Chrysler, MCI and WorldCom, Quaker Oats and Snapple.

Sun executive vice president of Corporate Development and Alliances, Brian Sutphin, offered his view of why so many of the acquisitions he has been responsible for have been successful. He has one criterion that applies to every acquisition whether the purpose is to round out a product line or expand into new markets: "the quality of the people."[36] Under Sutphin's leadership, key acquisitions have brought world-class people and industry-leading products and technologies to Sun, including StorageTek,

---

35 Herb Greenberg, "Is the New Sears CEO a Joke?" http://www.cnbc.com/id/41754681/ (accessed February 2011).

36 Oracle, Sun Executive Boardroom "Mergers & Acquisitions: Strategies and Outcomes" 2006. http://www.sun.com/emrkt/boardroom/newsletter/1106leadingvision.html (accessed February 2011).

See Beyond, SevenSpace, Waveset Technologies, Kealia, Pirus Networks, and Afara Websystems. During 2011, companies such as Google and Facebook are buying startups, just to get access to their founders and employee talent.

The large mergers that have been successful—Bell Atlantic with GTE [Gran Tierra Energy, Inc.], now Verizon; Exxon and Mobil; and Price Waterhouse with Coopers & Lybrand became PricewaterhouseCoopers, now PwC—were able to hit the ground running and continue to grow because of their common respect for the workforce. About PricewaterhouseCoopers, observed Rick Telberg of *Accounting Today* the following year, "Normally we'll see layoffs, a winnowing of [service] redundancies, and a hiring slowdown with the pickup of business. None of that happened."[37]

Notice a pattern? Valuing talent makes the difference.

The Regulatory Perspective

As accounting reporting models move from GAAP to IFRS toward human capital financial reports, a few changes have occurred on the regulatory side (government). In this progression, the steps taken have been reactionary (after the horse is out of the barn), and have not gone far enough toward addressing the root causes of the problems or enough toward meaningful change.

The first related regulatory shift administered by the Securities and Exchange Commission occurred in 2002 after Enron, Worldcom, and other corporations exploded with fraud scandals throughout the 1990s. The new set of regulations, called the Sarbanes-Oxley Act (SOX), aimed for corporate accountability and prescribed penalties for wrongdoing. SOX basically made CEOs personally responsible for disclosures and decisions of the company. CEOs could potentially go to jail.

---

37 Kim Girard, PricewaterhouseCoopers merger pays off." *CNET News*, January 4, 1999. http://news.cnet.com/PricewaterhouseCoopers-merger-pays-off/2100-1017_3-219662.html#ixzz1FaZmAkqG (accessed February 2011).

The second regulatory measure came along in 2010. The Dodd Frank Wall Street Reform and Consumer Protection Act came about as the result of the practices that led to the bankruptcy and demise of Lehman Brothers in 2008 (the largest bankruptcy in US history) and the resulting financial meltdown that brought about the loss of eight million jobs. The new bill was put in place also to improve accountability and transparency, as well as to end American taxpayer bailouts of companies that are "too big to fail."

The Dodd-Frank bill actually doesn't do enough to address the Wall Street practices that created the large-scale problems in the first place. The reason is that those practices were designed to maximize short-term profits (mortgage bank securities, derivatives) and create higher stock prices in the short term so that all the millions of dollars in bonuses could still be paid.

The new bill was an attempt to reign in unscrupulous practices by putting more controls around the financial institutions. But this is dealing with the symptoms—out-of-control CEO compensation, obscene banker bonuses, and poor business control practices—not the cause. The cause is directly linked to our current financial reports' primary emphasis on short-term results versus long-term investments in talent that truly drives success in a business.

The newest regulations aren't doing anything to reduce unemployment rates, nor were they meant to. The current financial state of the US economy and the current regulatory laws are both exacerbating unemployment. Even when the economy improves and unemployment drops, there is a "new normal" predicted for the unemployment rate. According to the Federal Reserve Bank of San Francisco, the "new norm" may be 6.7 percent (rather than the 5 percent that economists used for decades to say was normal).[38] Chairman of the Board of Governors of the Federal Reserve System Ben Bernanke agreed with economists and policy makers who predicted

---

38 Annalyn Censky, "The 'new normal' unemployment rate: 6.7%." *CNN Money*. http://money.cnn.com/2011/02/14/news/economy/fed_unemployment/ (accessed 2/11).

that the unemployment rate is likely to stay high for several more years. This underscores the importance of adopting a new set of regulations to address unemployment.

In a worst-case scenario, high unemployment could push those people who have been out of jobs for too long to their tipping points (More than 44 percent have been without a job for at least six months[39]). San Francisco Federal Reserve executive vice president John Williams and research associate Justin Weidner pointed out that one of the factors of the "new norm" in unemployment (along with the housing "double-dip" and related mortgage problems, impediments to rapid relocation, and reduced incentives to seeking less desirable jobs) is that there is a "mismatch between workers' skills and what employers are looking for." This makes attention to the human capital supply chain critical to every company.

As we talk about the shifts in financial reporting from GAAP to IFRS to HCFR—in parallel to the regulatory rules that affect those reports—we have to evolve our regulations and laws again from 1) Sarbanes-Oxley Act, to 2) Dodd-Frank Wall Street Reform, to 3) regulations that addresses unemployment and the risk of larger recessions in the future.

The types of regulations that are needed must be proactive—not reactive. We can't wait for explosions and then apply Band Aids. Regulations need to be simplified and focused on reinforcing, encouraging, and optimizing employment growth. Companies that want to take a proactive human capital-focused approach are required to shift their reporting models. The human capital supply chain focus does address unemployment, and the human capital financial report model is proactive.

The health of companies and nations in the long term is contingent upon their willingness to invest in talent. If we continue on with a short-term focus, unemployment rates will continue to be high. *People* have the innovative ideas that drive businesses. So the ques-

---

39 Ibid.

tion is: How do we do a better job of matching people and talents with the jobs we need them to do? The human capital supply chain is based on the critical principle of matching talent with company needs in a real-time and ever-changing business world.

Within corporations, there are departments that are short-term oriented and departments that are long-term oriented. New departments have come about as a natural evolution that occurs when companies go from tactical approaches about business to more strategic focuses.

Companies had **sales** departments, which had a short-term focus (What did you sell today?). Over time, **marketing** departments were developed to create strategies to complement what sales departments do, and to take a look at tomorrow, but with a long-term strategic focus.

Companies had **accounting** departments that were short-term focused, keeping track of cash, assets, and liabilities on a day-to-day basis. The same evolution was necessary. Accounting is all about learning the rules for reports that are focused on the past. Accounting needed a partner to look at the future long-term aspects—so **finance** departments were formed to look ahead, use regression analysis, and figure out how much cash a company would need looking out into the future. Finance people didn't need to learn all the GAAP rules (depreciation, etc.); they needed to look to the future.

Human resources has arrived at this same crossroads. Most HR departments continue to be transaction-focused (handling the day-to-day, payroll, benefits, and lawsuits). But as HR moves from a tactical to a strategic focus, workforce planning departments have made some efforts to prepare for the future, but largely these efforts have not been strategic or focused on the **human capital supply chain**. A new human capital supply chain department is needed to be involved in the optimization of the organizations' global workforce, to provide that balance: look at the long term, be future oriented, make future-looking projections based on the analytics

(Ex. In three months, you will need to hire X; in six months you will need to hire Y).

Evidence based upon research by the **Sears Holding Group** suggests that there are actually two different types of people, with two types of personalities, appropriate for these differing roles. The traditional HR-focused person "reacts" to information ("I have three open requisitions I need to fill today"). The complement to this person is forward looking ("How many people will we need in six months?"). Company operations need both types of people and two types of departments. The first is the transaction-based department that includes traditional human resource responsibilities; the second group is focused on optimizing the mix of human capital, and is forward-looking. The first employees to populate such a department are most likely some of the forward-thinking workforce development people.

No company in the United States, as of 2010, had a human capital supply chain department. The accountability of this department entails looking at the current workforce situation and using calculation models to try to predict what is going to happen; analyze streams of data and develop predictive models (similar to the way meteorologists determine forecasts with the use of trends, patterns, and related weather data). But further, when forecasting what will happen, the human capital professional must also be able to predict the severity of the future situation. Using the weather metaphor, we know there will be precipitation, but do we expect a sprinkle or a hurricane? This type of information is invaluable to the CEO, executives, and investors.

Similar to meteorology, new human capital supply chain information is constantly pouring in. The human capital department must make sure that the HCSC (the flow of people in an out of the company) is optimized with the help of continually updated forecasts and human capital financial reports that look at all the information in the human capital supply chain to optimize their talent.

An example to more clearly connect the value of detailed analysis with operational reality can be seen in the airline industry. Airlines spend a great deal of money forecasting fuels costs. The average cost of a cross-country airline ticket in the United States was $506 in early 2011[40] ($33 profit and $473 total "costs"). Within the "total" costs, direct/employee labor ($95), and nonemployee labor/contingent workers ($32), which equals ($127) 27 percent of total costs. US airlines have developed sophisticated fuel hedging/buying departments in order to minimize the fuel costs to $98 per ticket. However, there is NO similar human capital supply chain department devoted to "optimizing" the cost of all labor at $127 per ticket, which is in this case is 30 percent higher than the fuel costs. Keeping the focus on the cost of fuel, and ignoring the people costs, is a missed opportunity. Similarly, food companies develop global commodity pricing models, and energy firms develop complicated exploration models.

The creation of sophisticated human capital supply chain models requires a new generation of human capital professional. The new human capital professional must understand the evolution of HR metrics. Instead of developing reports that are historically oriented (cost-per-hire, time-to-hire, turnover percentages, etc.), the new evolution results in **human capital analytics** that look to the future to help make better decisions. Consider: Reports are pure data—> Metrics are comparative—> but Analytics are optimized, looking at the future to help make decisions. If, for example, you take a look at absenteeism: Ask how many people are absent (report)—> What percentage is that of the total company workforce (metric)?—> Tie this information to three or more variables (analytics), such as revenue for the day, to help make decisions about whether it pays to hire a temporary employee when someone is absent, etc.

For many companies there is a total disconnect between human resources functions and the stated goals of the company CEO. In fact, a study (conducted by Accenture, one of the top-five management

---

40 "Flight Patterns," Anne VanderMey. *Fortune*, March 21, 2011.

consulting firms[41]) of a thousand CFOs revealed a trend to create even less of a connection between human resources departments and company CEOs. Eighty percent of CFOs have been given greater responsibility within their organizations and, of those, 40 percent now have oversight of HR, creating yet another layer between HR and CEOs. This trend is indicative of the lack of understanding human capital analytics among C-level executives. This trend illustrates the desperate need for human capital financial reports, which are, in large part, the reasons that HR is not usually taken seriously enough by C-level executives.

> **For many companies there is a total disconnect between human resources functions and the stated goals of the company CEO.**

If the company CEO indicates an interest in three things only: 1) customer satisfaction, 2) revenue, and 3) profits (many CEOs have those or similar primary interests—though the order may be reversed), then the human capital professional must take all their processes and evaluate which, if any, of the HR department activities address any of those three goals. Much of what most human resources departments do on a day-to-day basis has no direct effect on customer satisfaction, revenue, or profits.

A company doing this analysis will find that employee satisfaction can have a big relationship to customer satisfaction. Turns out that happy employees tend to treat customers better (Who knew?). This new human capital supply chain information, backed up by human capital analytics and human capital financial reports, will improve any number of employee-related decisions. An example by Canada's largest credit union related to the percentage of unfilled positions: By evaluating which departments have bigger or smaller numbers

---

41 Cathy Missildine-Martin, SPHR, "Using Analytics to Make the Right HR Investments," IQPC [International Quality & Productivity Center] HR Metrics Conferences, Chicago, February 17, 2011.

of open positions, a company was able to identify a direct relationship to revenue. If the staff was short of salespeople, the company was also short on revenue. Armed with that information, the human capital professionals could determine the right number of salespeople needed in place to meet or exceed revenue goals. Decisions to be made about hiring temporary staff could be made in real time with real numbers.

In another example **at that same Canadian credit union**, workers were asked the common questions about whether they felt they had the tools they needed to do their jobs. The company was able to demonstrate with human capital analytics that there was a direct relationship between how workers answered this question and the company's profitability. Turns out—> without the correct tools and equipment, the cost of running the department was much higher than if the investment had been made in the appropriate tools in the first place.

A human capital supply chain department is able to demonstrate correlations, develop human capital metrics and *prove* whether there is a relationship between the goals of the company and the efforts of the human resources department. HR metrics must be tied into what is most important to the business and not just what is important to HR.

Those three concepts (customer satisfaction, revenue, and profitability) turned out to be linear. The more focus put on one led naturally to the others. Focus on customer satisfaction produced more revenue, which in turn produced greater profitability. This information may wake up the large number of US firms that place profitability as their number-one focus and goal.

Customer satisfaction —> better revenue —> better profitability

4 Emerging Perspectives of Regulators and Authorities

THE PARTICIPANTS: THE FOLLOWING DESCRIBES THE roles of the key influencers and authorities involved in the process of approving and implementing a change in the financial reporting arena.

Securities and Exchange Commission (SEC): "The mission of the US Securities and Exchange Commission is to protect investors, maintain fair, orderly, and efficient markets, and facilitate capital formation."[42]

Society for Human Resource Management (SHRM): "The Society for Human Resource Management (SHRM) is the world's largest association devoted to human resource management."[43]

Financial Accounting Standards Board (FASB): "Since 1973, the FASB has been the designated organization in the private sector for establishing standards of financial accounting that govern the preparation of financial reports by nongovernmental entities."[44]

---

42 http://www.sec.gov/about/whatwedo.shtml.
43 http://www.shrm.org/ABOUT/pages/default.aspx.
44 http://www.fasb.org/jsp/FASB/Page/SectionPage&cid=1176154526495.

The Big Four (auditing firms):
1) Deloitte Touche Tohmatsu Limited (DTTL)
2) PricewaterhouseCoopers International Limited (PwCIL)
3) KPMG International Cooperative (KPMG)
4) Ernst & Young Global Limited (EYG)

We will demonstrate how this new concept of HCFR waterfalls through government and business, and show the interrelated roles of the various participants and rule-makers that are typically involved in regulatory changes within the financial arena. From federal or state government legislation, new change filters through the SEC toward implementation with the assistance of FASB and SHRM.

1) FASB accountants provide interpretations of the new change and give guidance to the Big Four. From there, procedures are developed to verify the interpretations, focusing on the processes and determining if things are flowing properly.
2) SHRM then interprets the new regulations from a human capital point of view and provides guidance to C-level executives and HR professionals.

Starting this book, a premise was made that there would surely be consistency of thought and discussions throughout the SEC, FASB, and SHRM. What we found, with dogged research efforts to find out for sure, was that these bodies are far behind in their understandings and discussions about these new HCFR concepts. The simple evolution from GAAP to IFRS is consuming them for the time being and they are unable to even look beyond this IFRS transition to consider better concepts. As these groups come up for air, they will be able to more readily see the drastic evolution that is currently occurring around them. In the meantime, the time is ripe to present the HCFR message to politicians, corporate leaders, and investors to start the process of refining the nature and purpose of human capital financial reports, so that regulators can ultimately implement them.

Securities and Exchange Commission (SEC)

One of the biggest challenges for the Securities and Exchange Commission is that they are being given more and more responsibility in the financial world. Yet, they have a relatively small budget[45] (1.4 billion dollars/about 1 percent) as compared to what the US government spends ($1.2-$1.4 trillion annual budget).

The SEC issued a proposed "roadmap" in **November 2008** for a path toward the adoption of International Financial Reporting Standards (IFRS) in the United States and published no other announcements about this effort until **February 2010** when a statement was made in support of the IFRS as the best positioned reporting system to be a single set of "high-quality global standards." Further analysis was planned for the next year regarding the potential to incorporate IFRS into the US public market. A work plan was designed to consider the implications of the change, including developing and applying IFRS to US reporting systems, independent standard setting, investor understanding and education, effects on current US regulations, impact on all users (changes to contracts, governance, litigation contingencies), and readiness of human capital reporting.

The SEC committed to providing regular public updates on the progress of the work plan and they made their first update in **October 2010**, which reconfirmed their commitment to have a decision sometime during 2011 regarding the implementation. Stay tuned!

SEC Chairman Mary Schapiro said in **December 2010** that the Dodd-Frank Act would not influence the IFRS decision, and that any transition to IFRS would take a "minimum of four years."[46]

If this timeline is carried out, and the decision is made to incorporate IFRS into the US reporting system, the first reports under that

---

[45] http://www.washingtonpost.com/wp-dyn/content/article/2010/02/01/AR2010020102378.html.

[46] "IFRS: Current situation and next steps," pwc. December 2010. http://www.pwc.com/us/en/issues/ifrs-reporting/transition-to-ifrs-status.jhtml (accessed March 2011).

system will occur on or after **2015**, with staggered implementation dates thereafter. The SEC statement in **February 2010** referenced possible early adoption and a potential choice between IFRS and GAAP. They will continue to evaluate the timeline, but I will not hold my breath.

Financial Accounting Standards Board (FASB)

Since 1973, the FASB has been the designated organization in the private sector for establishing standards of financial accounting, which govern the preparation of financial reports by nongovernmental entities. Those standards are officially recognized as authoritative by the SEC and the American Institute of Certified Public Accountants (AICPA). Such standards are both important to the efficient functioning of the economy because decisions about the allocation of resources rely heavily on credible, concise, and understandable financial information.

The SEC has statutory authority to establish financial accounting and reporting standards for publicly held companies under the Securities Exchange Act of 1934. Throughout its history, however, the SEC's policy has been to rely on the private sector for this function to the extent that the private sector demonstrates the ability to fulfill the responsibility in the public interest.

The mission of the FASB is to establish and improve standards of financial accounting and reporting that foster improved financial reporting (by nongovernmental entities) that provides decision-useful information to investors and other users of financial reports. That mission is accomplished through a comprehensive and independent process that encourages broad participation, objectively considers all stakeholder views, and is subject to oversight by the Financial Accounting Foundation's (FAF) Board of Trustees.

The FASB is part of a structure that is independent of all other business and professional organizations, which includes (in addition to the FASB) the Financial Accounting Foundation (FAF), the

Financial Accounting Standards Advisory Council (FASAC), the Governmental Accounting Standards Board (GASB), and the Governmental Accounting Standards Advisory Council (GASAC). As part of this structure, FASB encourages conferences and discussion about new trends, such as the impending change from GAAP to IFRS reporting standards.

FASB hosted a panel discussion at a Town Hall Los Angeles conference in late 2010 to discuss the potential transition by US companies from US GAAP to International Financial Reporting Standards (IFRS).[47] Some companies expressed dread concerning the transition. Brent Woodford of Disney called it "a nightmare."

Voiced concerns included:

- GAAP is based on "rules" issued by the Financial Accounting Standards Board but IFRS is based on "standards," requiring more judgment on the part of accountants, making possible inconsistent interpretations that could lead to more lawsuits.

- Cost of the transition to a new system.

- Renegotiating contracts and covenants originally agreed to be based on GAAP reporting.

- How disagreements about the standards would be handled under the new system.

Advantages noted included:

- The change is inevitable.

- More than one hundred countries already use IFRS.

- Multinational companies will save money by using one system.

---

47 Citation: "A Financial Y2K In 2012?"*CNBC*. http://www.cnbc.com/id/27702796/site/14081545 (accessed March 2011).

- Convenience of everyone in the world reporting in the same format.
- IFRS gives investors a better picture of a company's true finances.
- While GAAP seems easier for accountants (follow the rules and plug in numbers), rules and numbers can be manipulated. By adhering to principles of IFRS, a more truthful picture can emerge.

Society for Human Resource Management (SHRM) and the Big Four

Parallel to the SEC work on figuring out what they want companies to report, the Society for Human Resource Management, the largest global association for human resources management, kicked off an "Investors Metrics Work Group" in 2011—pulling together experts from around the country to create recommendations and present them through the American National Standards Institute (ANSI) and the International Standards Organization (ISO).

Dr. Lauren Bassie, an independent consultant who is the chair of this work group, is an industry expert who has for years been analyzing the relationship between company performance and human capital metrics. Dr. Bassie's own work on stock portfolio analysis compares company performance and HR metrics, and analyzes how they move together. She contends that human capital ratios strongly correlate to financial performance. There is truth to the fact that what a company does with their employees and their workforce does directly correlate to a company's financial performance.

In the past, some have balked that there is such a relationship, but now we know for a fact that there is—there is evidence. And there is evidence that some form of human capital financial reporting is needed and eagerly anticipated by the global investment community. The work being done by SHRM is an example. In 2010, SHRM partnered with the American National Standards Institute and the International Standards Organization to tackle the nagging problem of reporting inconsistency. Currently, companies around the world have different definitions for turnover, cost-per-hire, time-to-hire, and many other HR-related metrics that have been used by executives for the last fifty years. HR professionals, investment lawyers, and thought leaders from around the world began sharing their ideas and experiences to help develop human capital metrics that could be used consistently across corporations anywhere.

Having joined the SHRM Investor Metrics Workgroup in early 2011, I became involved in the proposed formulation and standardization of these long-overdue and more-consistent human capital metrics. The workgroup was divided into four teams to approach all aspects of this endeavor. Initial charters included: 1) Research Discovery Team to explore the most relevant HR metrics, 2) Human Capital Indices Team to narrow down the wide breadth of metrics to the "top two–five indices," 3) "Getting Standards to Stick" Team to plan out the actual promotion efforts, and 4) Related Discovery Team to seek out and coordinate with other international organizations. Any standards recommended by the SHRM Workgroup will require the approval of the SHRM director of Standards before being passed to the American National Standards Institute (ANSI), and eventually passed forward to the International Standards Organization (ISO) for final approval and global implementation.

A convergence of thought is occurring within this group and around the world—something that happens whenever new ideas evolve. Like scientific breakthroughs, these new concepts typically don't come into being through the efforts of a single person. People in different places come to an idea with different thoughts and approaches—each approaches it from different angles. With all new ideas, breakthroughs, and innovations, people document what they are doing, read and watch the work of others in their field of interest, and collectively come to a conclusion—whether it's a new idea, a new technology, a new surgical procedure, or a new innovation. Implementation is then possible because each participant can share their viewpoints, share their research, and assist in creating one unified thought.

This process is exciting and very different from the way innovations came into being as little as fifty years ago—when these things happened so much more slowly. Researchers mailed their ideas back and forth among each other, depending upon the postal service, and possibly engaged in phone conversations and conferences. When experts from widely diverse geographic areas finally came to agreements of any kind, it was then a much harder and slower process to disseminate the information to the rest of the world, perhaps though conferences, professional journals, or other media outlets over time.

As the SEC, FASB, SHRM, and other interested parties in the financial arena bring ideas together, innovation will happen faster. Pulling together ideas around the human capital financial reports and human capital metrics/analytics can be disseminated to all interested parties with a click of a mouse.

The Common Thread

The common thread between all of these interested parties is that the United States and the world need a single, more-consistent financial reporting method that is global—but one piece is still missing. GAAP and IFRS make only a two-legged stool. GAAP contributed consistency and IFRS made it global, but to make it work we need the third leg; human capital financial reporting is needed to address and insert the human capital aspect that makes the difference in corporate valuation and corporate performance.

In order for all three ideas to be used—for there to be appropriate rules, procedures, and practical applications—the SEC, FASB, SHRM, and the Big Four audit firms must come together. The SEC has to define the processes from a legislative and administrative point of view. FASB must define the reporting standards. SHRM must (working with corporations around the globe) disseminate information from a human resources and operational point of view. The Big Four can then imbed these ideas into their audit procedures. Ideally, each body is helped by the other—the way the conversion of ideas into implementation has always worked—all concerned bodies working together toward a common purpose and a common passion.

However, in spite of the best intentions, these efforts can be stopped by self-interests and lobbyists. In 2009, about 130 German corporations and organizations worked on developing a set of human potential indices (HPI) and collected an impressive amount of information which proved that greater than 40 percent of a company's financial success can be directly tied to the successful management of human capital.

After the HPI metrics were developed, Germany's largest corporations stopped the efforts because they argued that the reporting of these HC metrics would cause an "administrative burden"; creating HR metric uniformity would "constrain human capital innovations"; and reporting intangible assets was risky and inappropriate.[48] These reasons appeared to the implementation committee as a smokescreen created by some big corporations that did not want to tell their investors about the performance of their workforce.[49] This "German syndrome" will probably be just as strong in the United States.

Changes to any age-old process, especially a process related to money, can be very difficult to implement. Even with a growing global demand for corporate and government transparency, getting many different parties to agree on a new way of thinking about organizational success and changing our reporting habits is an ambitious quest. Even with the "convergence of thoughts" combined with supporting research, the passion and determination to drive forward with these new ideas and reporting formats are necessary. This "string

---

48 Achim Sieker, Federal Ministry of Labour and Social Affairs, Germany. "Human Potential Index: Lessons Learned," MAM Meeting, April 13, 2011.

49 Ibid., SHRM Investor Metrics Workgroup phone call conference, April 11, 2011.

of intention" surrounding human capital financial reporting will continue to be strongly challenged. Lobbyists and special-interest groups will without a doubt try to derail these changes and destroy these efforts, but this revolution will not be crushed.

5 Birth of Human Capital Financial Reports

IN 2010, AS *HUMAN CAPITAL FINANCIAL REPORTS* WAS being developed as the second book in a trilogy, the previously referenced "convergence of thoughts" was already in evidence in the conversations at The Conference Board meeting on HR Metrics in San Diego, California. Others share my passion for changing the face of the human resources function to make business more efficient throughout the corporate world. The support for this "string of intention" is found in books such as *Entering the Human Age: Thought Leadership Insights* published by Manpower, Inc (2010), in a 2011 white paper by Jeff Higgins of the Human Capital Management Institute called "Human Capital Financial Statements," and among the Investor Metrics Workshop members at SHRM.

Standard GAAP formats

As thought leaders share their concepts at conferences and over the Internet, a review of the basic structure of financial reporting formats is in order. These individual financial reports are, to the detriment of investors, stuck in the past. To illustrate specifically why reporting traditional GAAP statements for companies must be changed to accommodate the new knowledge economy, this section draws attention to the failings of the most typical line items in current financial recording and highlights the problems with the four key financial statement formats. The premise for how human capital financial reports can correct these problems will be obvious. Once you are sufficiently convinced of this reasoning, the specifics will be outlined in detail with a chapter for each of these four standard GAAP formats and an introduction to the equivalent, more useful counterpart format in human capital financial reports. We begin with simplified definitions used throughout the book for these standard terms.

Profit and Loss Statements (P&L)

Profit and loss statements look at what short-term profits are made over a given period. The primary focus is on the short term and the information gleaned is historically based. The main fallacy in P&L statements is that they take the concept of human capital and absorb it into typical "expense" categories such as the following:

Costs of goods sold (COGS): These numbers are the results of taking all the direct material and all the direct labor costs and smushing them together. In the old industry economy, where inventory was large and labor was a small part of the overall costs, that approach made sense. In a knowledge economy, that approach no longer makes sense because the cost of labor has risen significantly and the cost of materials has dropped in most cases.

Sales and marketing (S&M): In an industry economy, this category included advertising and marketing materials; and, again, the people costs are buried within this expensive category, creating a distorted picture of the true cost.

Research and development (R&D): The same dynamic is found here; the people costs are smushed together with expensive equipment and research lab costs. The significant people cost is entirely lost and under-accounted for.

General and administrative (G&A): In this case, rent, utilities, legal costs, and people costs are smushed together (once again).

In all of the above GAAP categories, there is no way to know how much is being spent on just the company workforce. C-level executives, as well as stockholders and investors, cannot tell what percentage of the total company expenses are people-oriented. Is it fifty-fifty? Sixty-forty? How could you know? This information is vital as we move from an industry-based economy to a knowledge-based economy, because the percentage of people costs has risen so dramatically. That a company's CEO might have no idea of the actual percentage is the key problem with the current use of P&L statements. They perpetuate the ongoing, limited, short-term focus on profit that is the crux of the failure of current financial reporting practices.

Balance Sheet

The balance sheet reflect a snapshot on a particular moment that explains what the value is of what you own (assets) and what you owe (liabilities). These forms are set up to report three categories: assets, liabilities, and equity. Nothing is reported as to the value of the workforce.

Assets: Assets are considered to be the value of the historically recorded fixed items that depreciate over time. That matters in an industry economy. But the same problem is seen here because this valuation does not take into consideration the specific value of people. In a knowledge economy, the bulk of assets are people-related. Considering "assets" that are not inclusive of people is backwards. People don't depreciate; in fact, as workers gain more experience and training, the value of talent to a company actually appreciates and increases over time—but this is not considered.

Liabilities: This section on the balance sheet only looks at those items that a company owes money to those outside the corporation (creditors, vendors, etc.). This ignores what the company owes internally—which is often unrecorded and can be quite substantial over time. Examples include unfunded pensions, unfunded payroll taxes, accrued vacation, etc., that will eventually come due and must be paid.

Another type of "liability" that is not typically recorded that relates to the company workforce includes lawsuits that are a result of discrimination, EEOC, or Workers' Compensations claims. Companies do not insert those amounts onto their balance sheets until the amount is known for sure, when the case is finally settled, which can be after a period of years or even decades. But eventually that "boom" will likely drop. In this regard, how does a potential investor (interested in buying or investing in a company) understand the true total liabilities of a company?

Wouldn't it be far safer and "good business" to insert some reference to such "unrecorded liabilities" and potential liability amounts of that sort—something along the lines of "What's the most we could lose? And how will we cover that loss if or when it occurs?

Equity: This section on a balance statement shows how much a company owns minus how much the company owes—that difference is called "equity." And again, people costs are not reflected in these numbers. Equity statements are entirely meaningless in a knowledge-based economy because of all the things not taken into account or outlined. Such a record might not be needed moving forward with the use of human capital financial reports because the human capital financial reports reflect assets and liabilities in terms of people—all categories of worker (full-time, part-time, temporary, contract, and consultants).

Cash Flow

Cash flow has always been seen as the most critical page of the traditional financial statement. This report is compared to previous cash flow statements, and shows where the cash came from and where it went (how it was acquired and how it was spent). But the concept of what happens with cash over a period of time should not be the only measurement. The **flow of talent** has the most impact on the flow of cash. Talent generates the ideas; talent closes the sales that produce the cash. People are the number-one driving force behind a company's performance. That is the advantage of knowing why and how levels of talent change over time.

At the heart of the cash flow statement are all the activities of the workforce—the revenue generated per employee as well as the average human capital expenses incurred per employee. Understanding the balance/mix/and flow of talent categories, and optimizing that knowledge, is far more critical and essential to the long-term performance of a business. Attention to this talent flow and mix of talents will drive performance and the accumulation of cash.

Financial Ratios

Companies typically have a fourth page to their financial statements where financial ratios are listed, such as the percentage of profit as compared to revenue. Stock market experts and stock analysts look at these pages in particular to figure out the "financial health" of companies and which companies have the stronger potential for profitability and stock appreciation. Ratios normalize companies so that it is possible to compare large firms to small firms and across different industries and currencies. Even if the dollar amounts are different, it is possible to evaluate percentages from a comparative analysis point of view.

The financial world continues to rely heavily on these financial ratios, which analyze the other three pages of the financial statements to come up with quick answers to complicated questions. The problem (again) is that this method only looks primarily at short-term profits and doesn't look at all at the flow, mix, or importance of talent to the long-term financial health of a company. Human capital metrics offers a new way to evaluate the true value of a company by using human capital information that encompasses the unrecorded/ excluded workforce portions of a company's capital.

> **Human capital metrics offers a new way to evaluate the true value of a company by using human capital information that encompasses the unrecorded/excluded workforce portions of a company's capital.**

A New Age of Human Capital Analytics

All companies need a mechanism for better planning and forward thinking to forecast out further—to understand the talent mix they will need as the economy changes. There will be greater need for specific skills related to a knowledge economy that are not the same as within an industry economy. Whole new categories of people will be needed; massive retraining will be necessary to create the required global workforce.

We must look at future global workforce needs and take action now for the future. But this concept has no place and is not reflected in the GAAP financial statements still in use. Companies have typically looked out only over the current year. For many years, the healthcare industry has been looking out five to ten years to forecast the future availability of nurses. To address potential shortages, nurse recruitment is being carried out in high schools, and may well end up requiring grade school recruitment!

New human capital analytics will make the forecasting process much easier. The concept is a natural fit with staffing firms that have operated under a people-focused model all along. Staffing firms have the metrics because their survival and their revenue hinge on human capital analytics. The model they use to provide a pipeline of the five worker types to all sorts of companies is a pure science. Staffing firms have been ambitious organizations out of necessity; because, if they are not efficient in finding talent, assigning talent, and taking care of their customers, they will go out of business. (Corporations and recruitment departments feel no similar threat related to going out of business; if the department doesn't fill the open job requisitions, the human resources workers still keep their jobs.)

In the industrial economy, everyone was fulltime; there was only a tiny contingent workforce. But now, with the growth of the contingent workforce, staffing firms are well-suited to help corporations figure out what is affected by the flow of people throughout an organization. Because staffing firms pay detailed attention to the entire mix of the workforce, and create optimized mixes that are critical to companies, they ride the crest of the wave.

For C-level executives, stock holders, and investors, human capital financial reports offer a new way to look at the health of a company. HCFR provides valuable and useful insights into the true drivers of the performance of a company. More than at any time in the past, talent is the key to what truly drives the long-term growth and success of any organization.

> **More than at any time in the past, talent is the key to what truly drives the long-term growth and success of any organization.**

6 Structure of the Human Capital Financial Statements

Standard HCFR Formats

SIMILAR TO GAAP AND IFRS STATEMENTS, WE HAVE assembled a series of four human capital financial reports that reflect much more transparency concerning the importance of the workforce as it related to corporate performance. These four reports are designed to be intuitive to those executives and investors who are accustomed to the traditional GAAP-based accounting statements.

The formats of these reports are flexible in order to accommodate the varying needs of different businesses and different industries. Just as the IFRS statements make it possible to compare company financial statements across the globe, the human capital financial reports, although flexible, are also designed to drive global consistency. (Reporting formats need to reflect what is important to each individual company and industry, but must be globally consistent.)

Revenue and Human Capital Expense Statements (R&E)

Executives and investors need to better appreciate the direct relationship between the costs of their entire workforce and the entire revenue generated by that workforce for the organization. This must include all types of workers (full-time, part-time, temporary workers, contractors, and consultants).

Out of all the different relationships and trends that corporations must navigate, the relationship between the cost of the workforce and the creation of revenue is the single most important factor in overall corporate performance. That is why an entire financial statement is dedicated to this idea; of all the things we could look at (ratios, metrics, analytics), this is absolutely the most critical.

Human Capital Revenue

As with traditional financial statements, the proper recognition and reporting of revenue is essential, so of course, revenue is included in the human capital financial reports as well. A new distinction is made between upfront revenue and recurring revenue, since the mix can have a substantial effect on the performance and health of a company. In the knowledge economy, the creation of reoccurring revenues (more than one year in duration) is more valuable than the creation of one-time revenues. In most GAAP statements the type of revenue is not addressed or identified. All revenues are smushed together into one total.

The human capital financial report requires that the revenues be split out in order to demonstrate this distinction and manage the consistency of the revenue. Companies that don't distinguish between or report on one-time and recurring revenues are a riskier investment because there is no evidence that their revenue is consistent or reliable.

Human Capital Wage Expenses

Making a distinction between wage-oriented expenses and program-oriented expenses is important in order to understand the total wages being paid to all categories of workers—internal wages as well as external payments to staffing companies, contractors, and consultants. The number-one cost category in the knowledge economy is the human capital wage amounts for all five categories and all related workforce suppliers.

Human Capital Program Expenses

Human capital program expenses relate to company investments in the workforce. Wages represent dollars paid out to the workforce that are directly related to the generation of revenues. But human capital related program costs for workers represent decisions on the part of the company to invest in their workforce. These "program" costs include whatever percentage the company pays for employer-paid taxes, workers' health insurance, training, the costs for stock option plans, investments in wellness programs, etc. Companies must decide how much they want to invest in such programs, for we know that investment in those types of programs will result in a more engaged and productive workforce (a good reason to break out these costs).

Non-Human-Capital Expenses

Non-human-capital expenses are the other expenses a company has to pay that are traditionally included in the following four categories that we've been used to looking at with the people costs smushed together. But, by stripping out all the wages and program costs related to the workforce, we can see the remaining core costs in each of these areas:

Cost of Goods Sold will mean the cost of things like materials and utilities.

Sales and Marketing will mean the cost of things such as ads and trade shows.

Research and development (R&D) will mean laboratory supplies, lab space, utilities, etc.

General and Administrative will include office equipment, interest on debt, etc.

So, from revenue, we can deduct wages, deduct human capital programs, and deduct non-human-capital expenses and what is left over is the human capital "value" (i.e. profits) created by the workforce. The Revenue and Human Capital Expense Statement (R&E) essentially reformats the traditional GAAP P&L to more clearly identify all workforce costs associated with the human capital supply chain.

Talent Sheet

Assets

A talent sheet makes it possible to take a snapshot of the workforce to understand the makeup and mix of workers on any particular day. This category is broken into three parts:

1) Full-time workforce (making distinctions between executives, managers, professionals, and associates) who are generating revenue.

2) Contingent workers (how many and what types are adding revenue), who are developing new products, and supporting customers.

3) Non-workers (retirees receiving benefits, workers on leave or furlough, employees on strike) who are no longer currently adding to revenue. The reason they are included in the talent sheet is because they are a cost to the organization and they still represent a huge pool of talent with known experience and known skills. Companies need to keep tabs on this pool of workers, just like colleges who keep track of their alumni for years and years.

These workers are an existing, trained, and experienced part of the workforce that can be quickly reactivated to help generate revenue for the organization. In one city in California, more than 50 percent of the employees (250 of 450) had to be let go with little notice in order to save the town from bankruptcy. Everything changed overnight for those employees.[50] But those 250 workers did not disappear; many became contingent workers. Others moved down the supply chain to the non-worker category at that moment, drawing pensions or on COBRA. (No doubt some were later hired back as contingent workers without pensions and without benefits.)

The talent sheet is not a static document. Changes in the workforce are reflected, including the kinds of changes described in the California example. Without the human capital financial report, we wouldn't know where the cuts came from, especially because the human capital costs would have been smushed together in all the various other categories of costs (we couldn't see whether the cuts were made in the police department or the schools). With the human capital financial report, the taxpayers (investors) can see exactly what departments were reduced. This is helpful information for other institutions and organizations as well. For example, what about a state university that makes drastic budget cuts? State legislators and taxpayers need to know if they are letting go of administrative help or professors—not just the people, but the categories of people. The human capital financial report assures that critical transparency. Current annual report and 10-K reporting practices have not required this type of analysis of the changing makeup of the workforce.

---

50 http://www.msnbc.msn.com/id/42258668/ns/us_news-the_new_york_times/ (accessed March 2011).

Liabilities

Liabilities are the human capital risks related to the talent. These include unfunded or unrecorded costs related to the workforce (pensions, payroll taxes, unrecorded vacations) and these are the dollar amounts that don't show up in typical GAAP balance sheets. As baby boomers retire from companies and government organizations with generous pension plans, there is often no record of these significant headcounts. In some cases the retirees are a larger proportion of the workforce than the remaining working employees. Companies and investors need to be aware of this ratio of non-working employees compared to the entire company workforce.

Investors/taxpayers want and need to know about any unrecorded liabilities, such as pension plans—many of which are underfunded, or in a few cases are fully or over-funded. In some cases, companies are purchased/acquired and even raided for the express purpose of acquiring the cash in the company's pension plans. What happens to those workers who are let go before they are vested and reach retirement age? They don't get the pension money that the company has been funding during the person's employment! New owners of a "raided" company can lay off workers (in their forties, for example) and are free to keep any pension money that is not vested or fully vested. (Workers will get back their own money that they put into their pensions, but they won't ever see the amount the company put in during the years of their employment.)

Companies typically don't want to talk about their non-workers because it's such a huge issue (the silent workforce). In many cases, companies and local governments have not paid as much attention to the roles of retirees because they have no further influence over them. Yet this group is a very powerful, yet silent, part of the workforce. The liability owed to these retirees is becoming bigger and bigger. The sizes of their unfunded pension plans are large and getting larger, with the potential to put some companies and local governments out of business. These longstanding arrangements are part of the contract between the company/government and the workers, which has now become a trust that is often broken.

With human capital financial reports, a light can be shone on this growing issue because these non-workers are an increasing percentage of the population. In many cases the numbers are huge and represent a large unrecorded liability to companies and government organizations. Investors/taxpayers want and need to know what those hidden liabilities are and how large they are. These factors will affect the financial and human capital health of a company in the future because, when those liabilities come due, the company may be strapped for the cash. That same cash should have been invested in their workforce. Not having done so will affect the overall long-term financial performance of the company and the ability to further invest in the workforce (the people actually responsible for generating the company's revenue).

Equity

Equity is irrelevant in this case because in the financial world, equity is the difference between what you owe and what you own. This is meaningless when the focus is on the quality and quantity of the workforce. Companies don't "own" talent—workers don't belong to them.

Talent Flow

There are similarities between a talent "flow" sheet (cash flow) and a talent sheet (balance sheet). A talent sheet presents a picture of the entire workforce on a particular date. The talent flow sheet shows how the company got there over time. The sheet starts with the prior period (i.e. December of last year) and shows how many people have been added to the workforce, as well as how many have left or been terminated. This makes it possible to see the flow of talent over time.

When we know how many new hires we have, how many people left, and how many we had to terminate, executives and investors can use this information to evaluate the reasons and take appropriate corrective action. Did people leave due to bad performance or poor management?

Cash flow compares dollars—where they came from and where they went. This talent sheet does the same thing with people in the workforce. The unique part is that, based on those categories, you are able to also note how many unfilled openings there are at any point in time. Management and investors *need to know* that number of unfilled openings in order to understand if a company is expanding or shrinking its workforce and why.

Human Capital Metrics

Human capital metrics (instead of financial ratios) look at the other three statements to identify the most important percentage relationships to analyze more closely. Key items to examine may be, for example:

- The amount of revenue compared to the amount of human capital expense (R&E)

- The percentage of contingent workers in relations to the full-time workforce (Talent Sheet)

- The turnover (how many left on their own as a percentage of the entire workforce, and whether that number is moving in a particular direction (Talent Flow)

The real value here is to be able to know what happened this year, last year, and whether the workforce situation is getting better or worse. This page could evolve over time into human capital analytics, allowing for more projections and further analytical modeling concerning the future of the workforce.

The Purpose of Human Capital Financial Statement Metrics

In an industry-based economy, Enterprise Resource Planning (ERP) is critical, encompassing a plan for all the resources that go into building a product, e.g. the building of a car. But a knowledge-based economy is focused on the workforce (rather than products). When 50 percent of the workforce is contingent, it's more challenging to motivate those workers. The company has less control and, in many cases, the workers don't actually work directly for you. This requires companies to pay attention to different things, especially the new information presented in human capital financial reports.

Another **ERP** acronym can be used to describe what companies must better understand in a knowledge economy: the **E**NGAGEMENT, **R**ETENTION, and **P**RODUCTIVITY of their entire workforce.

Engagement refers to how satisfied workers are with their jobs (employee satisfaction). The better job they do, the better they will treat customers, which will result in greater revenue for the company. Eighty percent of workers may be relatively happy, but how do you make them as engaged as possible in their jobs?

Retention concerns those workers at the bottom of that engagement ladder and requires a look at flight risk. A worker's lack of engagement could be 100 percent the company's fault.

Productivity of those workers is dependent upon making sure they have the most advanced tools and techniques to do their jobs as efficiently as possible.

To have a great workforce you need to pay attention to those three things—each area needs to be of high importance. So, how do you achieve this type of optimized ERP with your workforce? Answer: You start distributing your four new human capital financial reports to all executives, managers, and employees (That's right—everyone).

7. Profit and Loss (P&L) vs. Revenue and Human Capital Expenses (R&E)

HCFR#1 REVENUE & HUMAN CAPITAL EXPENSES (R&E)

Report Dates	Current	Past	+/−
HUMAN CAPITAL REVENUES			
Product Revenues	$	$	$
Service Revenues	$	$	$
Recurring Revenues	$	$	$
Other Revenues	$	$	$
Total Revenues (1)	$	$	$
HUMAN CAPITAL EXPENSES			
Full-time Base Wages	$	$	$
Part-time Base Wages	$	$	$
Temporary Worker Expenses	$	$	$
Contractor (1099) Expenses	$	$	$
Consultant Expenses	$	$	$
Outsourced Labor Expenses	$	$	$
Wage Expense Subtotal (2)	$	$	$
Overtime	$	$	$
Commissions	$	$	$
Bonuses	$	$	$
Payroll Taxes (Fed/State/Local)	$	$	$
Health Insurances	$	$	$
Other Insurances	$	$	$
Training/Development	$	$	$
Recruiting/Relocation	$	$	$
Stock Option/Award Costs	$	$	$
401(k) Matches/Pensions	$	$	$
Wellness Programs	$	$	$
Program Expense Subtotal (3)	$	$	$
All Non-Human-Capital Expenses (4)	$	$	$
Total HC Value (1 minus 2, 3 & 4)	$	$	$

THE HUMAN CAPITAL FINANCIAL REPORT CONCEPT and the R&E statement in particular turns the focus on the talent you have in your organization and the cash investments made into that workforce over the last year or reporting period. This approach complements the current addictive short-term focus on quarterly earnings with a more balanced long-term focus on the workforce which is generating your revenues. Each focus (short-term earnings vs. long-term workforce) acts as a counterbalance to the other in terms of strategies, investments, and organizational goals. Instead of focusing exclusively on earnings per share, look at revenue per worker, and include all full-time and contingent workers in the calculation.

After thirty years as an accountant, CFO, and CEO, I've have concluded that, for the most part, **employees generate revenues, and executives generate expenses.** Even though you can always argue that these are not 100-percent rules, think about the decision processes that employees and executives follow on a daily basis. Employees (full-time and contingent) have the most direct impact on the creative development of new products and services, the mass marketing of those offerings, the closing of sales transactions, and the servicing of the customer base. Yes, employees can indirectly affect the amount of money spent to achieve those goals, but spending is usually tightly controlled by the monthly expense budgets that have been preapproved by management. It is during the annual budget cycle that the executives and managers of the organization truly determine the amount of money to be spent on revised marketing campaigns, new sales territories, as well as new investments in technology, headcounts, and infrastructure.

Human capital financial reporting makes it possible to evaluate how much is being spent on this workforce and how much the workforce is contributing to new and recurring revenues. This is not an investment in any one individual, but rather an investment in the entire workforce within the human capital supply chain, because there is a strong relationship between investments in the workforce and the resulting creation of revenues—the company's fuel for growth. We have already discussed in Chapter 5, the general structure of the 1) R&E statement, 2) Talent Sheet statement, 3) Talent Flow statement and 4) HR Metrics/Analytics. The next four chapters (Chapter 7 through Chapter 10) dive into detailed line items in each of these reports, and the reasons for restructuring your reporting with human capital financial reports.

Chapter 6, "Structure of the Human Capital Financial Reports," talked about the main sections of the R&E statement as the 1) Human Capital Revenues, 2) Human Capital Expenses (Wage & Programs), and 3) Non-Human-Capital Expenses. The net result of deducting the expenses from the revenues is human capital value added (HCVA), which is the same as GAAP NET profit. HCVA represents the amount of additional money that organizations can invest in worker wages, people programs, non-human-capital expenses, as well as stockholder dividends. These investment decisions are critical in order to generate future monthly revenues, especially in a knowledge economy.

Even though the NET amounts on the GAAP P&L statement and HCFR R&E statement are the same, there are two completely different sets of information being presented to investors, boards of directors, and taxpayers. In a knowledge economy, the HCFR R&E statement is a much better provider of relevant information related to the generation of revenues and the resulting human capital value for all those investments in wages and programs. There is a direct correlation between workforce investments and the generation of ongoing revenues.

R&E Human Capital Revenues

The revenue section of the R&E statement can be structured to match an organization's business and industry. Revenue streams are separated between one-time revenues and recurring revenues, but they can also be reported by geographic areas of the world. As companies and organizations move toward subscription-based monthly billing plans in order to smooth out their flow of revenues and cash across the year, they will be better able to predict, match, and manage their monthly revenues with their monthly flow of expenses.

A transition to the smooth monthly recognition of revenues has been a major reporting change for many industries, particularly the global software industry. As technology evolves and new ideas gain momentum, software companies and their customers have moved away from the large upfront purchase price for software and toward the rental of new web-based software applications. This rental revenue model, referred to as Software as a Service (SaaS), has transformed the software industry. This trend can be seen throughout our culture as more people lease cars rather than buy, and rent apartments instead of buying homes.

As with any evolution, some companies have been able to adapt, while others have filed for bankruptcy or been sold due to unpredictable changes to their revenue and cash flow. With the increase in online credit card payment plans and leasing opportunities, separating the types of revenues in reporting statements reflect a clearer picture of these shifting trends.

Another major distinction with the human capital financial report is the separation of service revenues from product revenues. Few businesses can sell a product in the global economy without a corresponding flow of service revenues. Even though some annual reports and 10-K supplements separate these different types of revenues, the information is usually buried in the back of the annual report. Because of the relationship between revenue recognition and workforce costs, those revenue details are inserted directly into the actual HCFR R&E report. In a knowledge economy, the percentage of revenues generated by recurring services and fees continues to grow as a percentage of total revenues.

The fourth and last category of HCFR revenue (product, services, recurring, and other) is "other revenues." As companies amassed large amounts of cash from improving revenues and capped workforce expenses at the end of the Great Recession of 2008–10, manufacturing companies as well as Wall Street bankers were able to generate large amounts on interest revenues (other). In many cases, companies avoided making critical investments in the workforce, in order to keep that interest revenue flowing. A Wisconsin appliance manufacturer (creator of the SaladShooter and the FryDaddy), National Presto Industries, accumulated so much cash that the SEC tried and failed to reclassify them as an investment bank, which would have required the manufacturer to adhere to more stringent disclosure rules.[51]

In the knowledge-based economy, the swings in these four types of revenue in the human capital financial reports can catch executives, investors, and politicians off guard. In the case of drastic revenue swings, the number-one benefit of implementing an optimized human capital supply chain is the ability to quickly synchronize the mix of a company's workforce (in real time) in direct relation to the mix of the organization's revenues. Directly connecting revenues to the size and mix of the workforce is not merely a human capital financial reporting requirement, but also an operational necessity.

Human Capital Wage Expenses

At the core of the HCFR model is the idea of bringing more attention to workforce-related expense details, because of the direct relationship with the generation of revenues. As we explained in Chapter 6, by separating human capital "wage"-related expenses from human capital "program"-related expenses, we see that changes in revenue typically cause changes in workforce wages, and that changes in program investments are typically controlled by corporate management decisions.

In the R&E report, a distinction is made between typical internal corporate payroll wages (full-time and part-time) and external contingent wages (temporary workers, contractors, and consultants) to illustrate the vast difference in the reporting and understanding of

---

[51] "National Presto wins assets case," *Milwaukee Wisconsin Journal Sentinel*, 5.17.07. http://www.jsonline.com/business/29351234.html (accessed June 2011).

these two categories in the eyes of internal executives and external investors/stockholders/taxpayers.

The R&E report calls specific attention to the amount of money spent on labor outsourced through external companies, including manufacturing plants to Mexico, entire HR departments to IBM, help desks to India, and development teams to China. These outsourced headcounts and their related expenses are distinguished from the employees receiving a direct paycheck from the organization. The corporation, nonprofit, university, or government organization is dependent upon these outsourced workers to generate revenues and provide services, but these costs and especially headcounts are often "kept off the books" by smushing their costs together with non-human-capital costs.

The reason for individual line items for those six categories of the workforce (including outsourcing) on the R&E report is that when moving through the Talent Sheet and Talent Flow reports of the HCFR, these same six workforce line items explain the headcounts required to run the entire organization, and how the mix of those headcount changes over time.

Human Capital Program Expenses

There is a complementary relationship between human capital wages and revenue generation that is just like the relationship between human capital program investments and workforce engagement. For years, organizations have taken for granted the dedication and engagement of their workforces. During the industrial economy of the past, full-time employees stayed with the same employer for their entire careers. But with the increasing mobility of the global workforce in a growing knowledge economy, organizations need to pay renewed attention to those human capital program investments that help recruit, retain, and reengage that workforce (the three Rs).

Overtime can be a great way to utilize experienced employees when unexpected revenues/workloads appear, and can also be used

Profit and Loss vs. Revenue and Human Capital Expenses 71

to reward existing employees with a bonus-like increase in pay. As a child, I remember my parents being so excited when my dad was asked to work overtime to help reconnect AT&T telephone lines after a storm. This meant our family could do some things (like take a vacation) that we couldn't typically do on a paycheck-to-paycheck lifestyle. My dad was motivated to seek out such opportunities on behalf of his family. This is the case with most families in the United States and around the world.

When overtime situations continue for extended periods of time, the organization must re-optimize its mix of workers to rebalance the workload between the appropriate worker categories. In an ideal world where the human capital supply chain is re-optimized on a weekly basis, overtime costs are minimized. Overtime costs monitored over months or even years can be one of the best indicators of a highly optimized human capital supply chain that is within controlled parameters.

Some companies try to control or even reduce commission costs; but in a growing business, commission investments are still a great way to motivate a hunter-mentality sales force (focused on new prospects) or a farmer-oriented customer account team (focused on nurturing existing relationships). The reporting and management of commissions as part of the R&E report is a great way for investors to see the amount of additional compensation paid to generate new revenues. Trends in commissions can also be an early warning signal for declining or rising revenues that should trigger an adjustment in the size of the required workforce.

In my own software company, we found that an "everyone sells" philosophy helps to expand the ability to earn commissions to every person within the workforce. That's right, everyone from the highest paid executive to an accounting clerk. Because the workforce is typically in the most direct contact with customers and prospects, we have found that the simple act of "listening to the customer or prospect" opens up buried revenue opportunities.

As an example, when an accounting clerk calls a customer about a past due bill, we often find that the customer is frustrated about something and they held their payment to get attention. If the accounting clerk is able to talk the customer into some additional training to solve the problem, the clerk earns the commission. The same holds true with support calls to our helpdesk, where a support tech can suggest additional services to the customer and receive the commission. You might think that our sales and account management teams would mind missing that small commission, but, in fact, this frees up the sales and account management professionals to be more proactive in pursuing bigger opportunities. When a workforce knows that every worker can earn a commission check, (we found) this energizes the entire workforce to higher levels of revenue generation.

Performance bonuses are also separated on the R&E report due to the spike or valley nature of bonuses throughout the organization. Investors and taxpayers can see if those bonus payments are actually backed up by exceptional performance. In those cases where bonuses have become automatic for executives regardless of actual performance, pressure from stockholders and the public can bring attention to unwarranted payments. (This usually happens when the board of directors finds an "unusual circumstance" to justify the unearned payment.)

Another form of bonus can come in the form of CEO "perks," which are now required to be disclosed in US annual reports and 10-K filings. Examples of bonuses that appear to be poor investments in CEOs during 2010 include:

- $724,000 for a car and driver for Jay Fishman (CEO at the Travelers Company)—what kind of car *was* that?

- $391,000 for personal tax preparation for Ray Irani (CEO at Occidental Petroleum)—that's more than most Americans even earn in a year!

- $216,000 for club memberships for Randall L. Stephenson (CEO at AT&T)—that's a lot of golf.

- $110,000 for an attorney to negotiate the compensation for Carol Bartz (CEO at Yahoo!)—is that a conflict of interest?
- Finally, $29,538 for a personal trainer for Martha Stewart (CEO at Omnimedia)—well, she is in shape!

On the other side of the coin, bonuses can be very motivating to any worker who goes above and beyond expectations to increase customer satisfaction, revenues, and/or net value. The key concept is for bonus programs to be available, equitable and transparent across all levels of employment, from the CEO to the janitor.

Even though the costs related to payroll taxes (federal, state, and local) are mandated by law, this category is showing signs of exponential increases, especially at the local level. As of 2011 there were more than nine thousand different local payroll tax jurisdictions across the United States, and many more communities use new local payroll taxes to help generate revenue. Ohio and Pennsylvania are the leaders in this race and between them account for over half of all local payroll tax jurisdictions.[52] In addition, these communities sign reciprocity agreements with neighboring communities to resolve local tax payments based on where a worker lives or works. As the federal government reduces the waterfall of tax-sharing payments with states, and as states shut off their payments to counties, and counties reduce their tax-sharing payments with cities and towns, the local communities will have to do something to maintain local services. These local payroll tax payments can be used to fund fire, police, schools, and roads, especially since it is so difficult to obtain voter approval to raise property taxes to support these services.

Of the most volatile human capital program expenses, health insurances lead the pack, especially as they relate to premiums for medical coverage and prescription drugs. As the baby boomer generation retires and the demand for healthcare services increase, the

---

52 Symmetry Software Local Tax Tracking, 2011. Customer information. www.symmetry.com.

costs of those services rise in unison. Combine that escalation in health insurance expense with the growing use of prescription drugs, and there is no end in sight for the ongoing increases.

Other insurance is separated from health insurance costs because of the unpredictable nature surrounding such expenses as workers' compensation insurance and unemployment insurance. Even though state governments controlled these program costs in the past, the current funding situation is completely different. In many states it is difficult to find workers' comp insurance and, if you do, the rates are high. In addition, most state governments have huge deficits in their state unemployment funds and have borrowed billions of dollars from the federal government. The states will probably need to raise unemployment rates on existing businesses to pay back these loans and refill their state funds. Because both of these human capital program costs have the potential to increase sharply after the recession ends, organizations need to report these program costs in more detail.

Earlier in this book, we talked about the shifting of training and development responsibilities from the expense of the organization to the shoulders of the worker. Even as this trend gains more momentum, organizations still provide certain "process training" that is specific to their operating procedures, especially with new hires. In addition, corporations and their investors will continue to monitor retention-based tuition reimbursement program costs, which may vary widely between corporations. Comparing the commitment to tuition reimbursement program expenses between similar companies is an early indicator to investors and new hires of a corporation's commitment to workforce development. Since training costs are typically the first expense to be cut in an economic downturn, this category on the R&E report can predict trouble to come.

The human capital program area of recruitment and relocation costs can help explain to investors and management the growing pains of the organization. When these costs are flat, then hiring and growth are expected to be flat for the organization. The costs for executive recruiters can easily hit 30 percent of a first-year salary, and background checks with E-Verify are becoming mandatory for every new worker. Even though the longstanding HR metrics of time-to-hire and cost-per-hire can be enlightening to executives concerning the productivity of their HR department, the true test is in comparing recruitment and relocation costs to changes in revenues. Because the purpose of recruitment is to find the "best talent" to drive revenues and the business forward, there should always be a positive correlation between paying for expensive headhunters and increases in revenue. If the recruitment costs stay high and revenue starts to decline, then stockholders need to question the return on those people-program investments.

This separate expense category is helpful when stock grants and stock options are awarded to executives for recruitment or retention purposes. Whether it is a huge stock award to a new CEO or a massive signing bonus to a baseball player, stakeholders will be able to see where the organization's net value is being spent. In recent years, these types of awards and grants have escalated beyond most of our imaginations, and yet the practice continues because managers argue that this is the price for hiring great talent. Some might argue that huge stock options are the only way to motivate executives to maximize earnings per share. Shrewd investors disagree with that argument, especially in an ever-expanding world of mobile global talent. The argument against these huge payments gets stronger and louder when we move away from profits and stock prices as the only defining measurement of corporate success. Again, the human capital net value of an organization and its ability to reinvest in its global workforce IS the best measurement of corporate success.

The human capital program cost line item of pensions/401(k) matches is another of those underfunded and politically charged subjects that has the potential for significant implications to corporations and government organizations. "The demographic picture looks different now that the baby boomers are starting to retire. In 1950 there were 7.2 people aged 20–64 for every person sixty-five and more in the OECD [Organization of Economic Cooperation and Development—representing thirty free-market countries]. By 1980 the ratio dropped to 5.1. Now it is around 4.1, and by 2050 it will be just 2.1. In short, every couple will be supporting a pensioner."[53]

Human capital financial reports bring crystal-clear attention to the amount being expensed on the R&E report as well as the amount of unfunded liability listing on the corresponding Talent Sheet. Those unfunded pension liabilities should not be refilled without first passing those expenses through the R&E financial report, rather than just moving cash around on the Balance Sheet. For many older companies, universities, and local governments with huge pension populations, this human capital program cost has the potential to bring these organizations to their knees over the next twenty years. The R&E demonstrates the magnitude of investments that will be needed to fully fund those plans. **Forewarned is forearmed.**

The last human capital program expense on the R&E report relates to all those traditional HR-related programs, including wellness, employee recognition, donations, counseling, picnics, discount programs, etc. Every organization has its own historical collection of such programs to help improve the morale and engagement of their workforce. Even though most of these programs were reserved for full-time workers, many of them have been expanded to include all categories of workers. In many HR organizations, these programs tend to consume a lot of HR time. Because of the desperate need for HR departments to become more strategic in their efforts, outsourcing these programs may be a consideration so that HR staff can move further away from transactional duties and more toward workforce optimization.

Non-Human-Capital Expenses

In most traditional financial statements, these industrial-based cost categories are grouped together as either cost of goods sold (COGS),

---

53 *The Economist*, April 19, 2011, p. 6.

sales and marketing (S&M), research and development (R&D), or general and administrative (G&A). When these four cost categories place the wrong emphasis on these old-school groupings, information is buried that would otherwise help executives and investors make better decisions. As we had explained in Chapter 6, concerning the structure of human capital financial reports, both human capital costs and non-human-capital costs are smushed together and presented in a GAAP or IFRS report as total spending for that particular department.

As depicted in our generic R&E report, non-human capital expenses can be reported as a single line item or it can be split into more traditional line items. For example, a manufacturer may want to separate COGS from the other three non-human capital categories because of the large amount of COGS expenses involved in their business. The whole point of human capital financial reporting is to reconstitute these GAAP reporting categories into just three: wage costs, human capital program costs, and non-human capital costs, which brings specific attention to human capital related expenses. This reformatting of the traditional P&L statement makes it possible for investors and analysts to compare the bottom line workforce performance of firms over time and across industries.

Human capital financial reports still maintain the GAAP, IFRS, and SEC rules surrounding the recognition of revenue, accruals for expenses, and the calculations for tax expenses. HCFR is not intended to change rules—only to change the reporting format so that previously omitted workforce information is brought to light. Accountants and investors can rest assured that the calculation of the R&E statement still produces the identical bottom line of the P&L. Human capital financial reporting is not taking away information; it is enhancing reporting in a way that provides everyone with more pertinent information.

Human Capital Value

This is the final line on the R&E report and it has a sister-like relationship with the more traditional concept of net profit. In an R&E report, the concept of human capital value primarily relates to the "net" revenue the corporation receives from the efforts of its workforce. Throughout this book, we have stressed the growing role of the extended workforce in achieving financial success and organization optimization. We have talked about what the workforce can bring to the organization in terms of revenues, new products, improved services, and customer satisfaction. In the knowledge economy, C-level executives provide strategic direction and investment decisions. The executive may be driving the bus, but the workforce is powering the engine. "Human capital value" is a much more appropriate term than "net profit."

Human capital value reinforces that the core driver of an organization's success is its entire global workforce and its ability to maximize revenues. The current addiction to earnings per share places the emphasis on what executives can do to reduce costs. The change in definition from "net profit" to "human capital value" shifts the primary success of the organization away from the board room and toward the workforce. This is the new definition of organizational success, which will result in more human capital value for stockholders and, in some cases, taxpayers. For the peace of mind of traditional investors and analysts, their stock models and analyses can now use human capital value as a replacement for net profit. As with net profit percentage, a human capital value percentage compares the amount of human capital value to total revenues as a stock performance indicator. The structure of the R&E statement is comprised of many pieces, but has a renewed focus on the true drivers of stockholder value, corporate success, and revenue growth.

8. Balance Sheet: Fixed Assets vs. Variable Human Inventory (Talent Sheet)

HCFR 2 TALENT SHEET (TALENT ASSETS & RISKS)

	Headcount on X date	% of Total Talent
HUMAN CAPITAL TALENT (ASSETS)		
Full-time Executives (P&L Responsibility)	#	%
Full-time Managers (Multiple Direct Reports)	#	%
Full-time Professionals (Degree)	#	%
Full-time Associates / Manufacturing (Non-degree)	#	%
Subtotal Full-time	#	%
Part-time Employees (Under 30 hours per week)	#	%
Temporary Employees (from Staffing Suppliers)	#	%
Contractors (1099)	#	%
Consultants	#	%
Outsourced Labor	#	%
Subtotal Contingents	#	%
Employees on Leave / Furlough	#	%
Employees Retired (Receiving Benefits)	#	%
Past Employees on Cobra	#	%
Employees On Strike	#	%
Subtotal Non-Workers	#	%
TOTAL TALENT AS OF (DATE)	#	100%
HUMAN CAPITAL RISKS ($$$ LIABILITIES):		
Unfunded 401(k) Match/Pensions	$	
Unpaid Payroll Taxes/Insurances	$	
Accrued PTO/Vacation Liabilities	$	
Potential EEOC/Wage & Hour/Worker Comp Fines	$	
Potential Discrimination/Employee Lawsuit Settlements	$	
Total Human Capital $ Risks	$	

BUSINESSES AND THEIR STAFFING ORGANIZATIONS have become lean and mean—this is the new normal—there is no slack in the system. But there are, and will continue to be, new challenges and growth opportunities, and each one will require improved enterprise resource planning (ERP). Being able to respond to these challenges and opportunities quickly and effectively is a new source of competitive advantage for corporations.

Current HR information systems were built around a steady state-type model—thinking of human beings as "assets," where they are treated as a fixed asset rather than fast-moving inventory. In the past, these fixed asset employees stayed with their organizations for their entire careers and were viewed as "lifers." This model does not work within the changing needs of the knowledge economy or the career habits of younger workers. To assess ever-changing needs (demand) and deliver just-in-time resources (supply) quickly, accurately, and with more flexibility, we must manage human capital resources as a *variable* cost rather than a *fixed* cost.

HCFR provides the tools to better manage the higher volatility, shorter time frames, and higher workforce transaction rates (more people coming in and going out at a faster pace). Inventory models have been optimized via supply chain planning and management—but people are not parts. People can walk out the door. That complexity must be considered when applying manufacturing supply chain concepts and disciplines to the unique requirements of human capital. The first book in this series, *Human Capital Supply Chains*, addressed that need in more detail while the HCFR Talent Sheet dissects and reports on the different categories of the flexible workforce.

As we walk through the generic human capital Talent Sheet format above, we see the global workforce separated between 1) full-time employees, 2) contingent workers, and 3) non-workers. All three categories represent "talent" in the form of experience, knowledge, and availability that can be tapped into, depending upon the needs of the organization and the workers. As this optimized workforce ratio reaches a fifty-fifty mix between full-time employees and contingent workers, organizations will have the cost benefits of a larger contingent workforce but there will be the corresponding risks that executives need to manage them differently. Non-workers, either direct (employees on leave) or indirect (retirees), represent a significant portion of a company's global talent pool—not just in their numbers and their potential for reengagement in the active workforce, but also the growing cost they represent to the corporation.

Full-time Workforce

The full-time employee category represents those employees that organizations are most capable of reporting on in their annual reports. Unfortunately, corporations are not "required" to report headcount mix numbers anywhere in their annual reports or 10-K filings. As a result, most organizations do not report any workforce levels, and investors are left in the dark concerning the size and mix of an organization's workforce. The antiquated reporting rules of the SEC and FASB do harm to stockholders by not helping them understand the makeup of the workforce. This is especially true of the "core" full-time workforce levels, as well as contingent and non-working employees. The categories of full-time employees include executives, managers, professionals, and associates.

We have separated the executive category from other management so that investors can evaluate the bench-strength of the executive team and how their numbers compare to the overall size of the organization. Stockholders and taxpayers will be able to see if an organization is "top heavy" in comparison to other similar organizations. Because certain titles, such as vice president, can be meaningless, especially in the banking industry where everyone seems to be a VP, we are focused on responsibility and not job titles. The executive category only includes those managers with complete P&L responsibility over an entire organization or division. Their compensation plans are usually more extensive and, in addition to base salary and performance bonuses, may also include stock options, severance contracts, and other perks. They typically include the "officers"—CEO, COO,

CFO, CSO, CMO, CHRO, and any other employees who have board-level responsibilities. Most annual reports and 10-K filings now include extensive required information about executive compensation programs. Human capital financial reports maintain this emphasis on the executive team, but we also expand the reporting to include the entire management team and others within the organization's human capital supply chain.

The management line item on the Talent Sheet represents those employees who have multiple (two or more) employees reporting to them in a department or division of some sort. This includes those individuals with responsibilities for achieving operational goals and handling the performance reviews for their subordinates. The size of the management team can limit the ability of an organization to take advantage of growth opportunities. This "growth capability" is helpful to stock analysts as they try to predict which organizations actually have the talent to expand into new geographies and manage the development of new products and services. The separate listing of executive and management headcounts on the Talent Sheet report makes comparisons possible with other similar organizations.

Full-time "professional" employees tend to be well educated with some type of college degree and are also likely to be well paid. This group, with their unique skills and intellectual property, has become the driving force for revenue growth for many firms in the knowledge economy. The creation of innovative new products, exciting new services, and strategic analysis is usually produced by this specific segment of the workforce. In many cases, outside contractors and consultants are brought in to augment the output of this group during large projects and heavy workloads.

The last worker category under the full-time heading is typically the largest group of an organization's workforce. These "associates" include those workers involved in manufacturing, distribution, retail, services, support, and a wide variety of other jobs. Because this group of full-time workers is large and less costly per person, it is typically the first group to be expanded during times of growth, and the first to be reduced during times of recession. This category is the most unionized of the full-time categories and also the least expensive in terms of both wages and human capital program costs. Because of the lower educational and experience requirements of the associate's work, this is the group that contingent workers can most easily complement during times of growth. In general, the full-time 1) executives, 2) managers, 3) professionals, and 4) associates of the organization currently represent the vast majority of most workforces. The changing global workforce trend toward more contingent workers will drastically reduce this full-time percentage of the total workforce over the next ten to twenty years.

Contingent Workforce

The part-time workforce is a fast-growing segment of the overall Talent Sheet workforce, especially as the baby boomer generation continues to retire. With workweeks kept below twenty hours per week, most human capital programs, such as health insurance and other benefits, are not offered to this group in the United States. In reaction to the retirement of seventy-eight million baby boomers in the United States, organizations are finding it increasingly effective to hire back recently retired employees as part-time workers in order to access to their knowledge and vast experience. Even though this group is typically paid through the organization's payroll department, they are separated on the Talent Sheet in order to draw specific attention to this growing segment.

To comprehend the enormity of that number (seventy-eight million), consider that there are only about 300 million people living in the United States and only about 200 million of them are available to work (kids and the elderly excluded). Removing those seventy-eight million workers from the 200 million total workers in the US human capital supply chain is a 39-percent reduction in the "supply" of US talent. That portends a significant impact on the US workforce in coming years. Many countries in Europe and Asia are also facing a similar daunting reduction in available workers in their long-term workforce planning.

With more than 2.5 million "temporary workers" in the United States (more than nine million worldwide as of May 2011[54]), this category is a large subgroup of the contingent workforce. In economies with high unemployment, especially among younger workers, many are taking temporary jobs as a way to get into the workforce and gain experience. In certain situations, corporations bring in a temporary employee to work for weeks or months before offering them full-time employment. This gives the organization a chance to see the person's work ethic, and it also gives the temporary employee a chance to see how desirable it is to work in the organization.

"Independent contractors" have become a preferred status for many workers in the United States and abroad. This category gives those professionals whose skills are in demand a flexible way to earn a living and maintain a self-directed work environment. From an organizational reporting point of view, this group is often neglected by human resource reporting because they are so difficult to track. In many cases, line managers and department heads are the ones (rather than HR representatives) who directly engage independent 1099 contractors, often without the help or notice to anyone in human resources. The contractor's invoice is often processed through accounts payable as an overhead expense, and no one at a corporate level knows how many independent contractors are running around their organization. Companies must be careful not to break co-employment laws, wherein long-term contractors are granted full-time benefits by the courts. To get around these laws, some organizations will bring a contractor in for about a year, let them go for a few months, and bring them back for another year.

Consultants are well trained, experienced, and usually available at a moment's notice. Because of their unique skills and availability, they can be very expensive, and are tracked through the Talent Sheet. As with contractors, consultants are often hired directly by managers

---

54 Richard Wahlquist, president and CEO of American Staffing Association (ASA) estimates 2.5 million per day in 2010, up from 2.01 million per day in 2009. About ten million individuals in total worked for staffing firms for some period of time in the United States over the course of 2010.

and executives to analyze or address a particular situation or opportunity. Because of this direct and sometimes secret engagement (ex. an effort to reduce the workforce, analyze a potential merger, etc.), the organization does not separately track their existence in numbers or dollars spent. How can anyone optimize a human capital supply chain of talent when a portion of that talent is hidden in the overhead costs?

In the Talent Sheet, the number of consultants and their costs are broken out and visible for the benefit of management, investors and taxpayers. In a government environment, consultants and lobbyists can cost significant amounts of money without working many hours. By including outside consultants, lawyers, and accountants together in this category, the organization can see and demonstrate the amount of talent it takes to actually run the organization.

The last category of contingent workers on the Talent Sheet includes all "outsourced" workers and departments. Outsourcing has gained in popularity over the last twenty years and continues to be an excellent way to spin off nonstrategic operations in order to reduce costs and add more workforce flexibility. A *Wall Street Journal* article[55] reported in May 2011 that "explosive growth in emerging economies is eating away at the cost advantage of outsourcing. The number of jobs US companies are bringing home from overseas is modest, but that could change. Wages are rising rapidly in China and other emerging economies that export to developed nations, while manufacturers in the United States have achieved significant productivity improvements while cutting costs."

The organization needs these outsourced resources to drive revenues, but their numbers are never reported and their costs are smushed with other costs. In order for management to understand the total number of human capital (bodies) it takes to run their organizations, they need to separate these workers on the Talent Sheet. On the other hand, corporations that *provide* these outsourced ser-

---

[55] John Bussey, "Analysis: Will costs drive firms home?" May 5, 2011, http://online.wsj.com/ (accessed May 2011).

vices will then report those same headcounts as part of their *full-time* employee totals.

The "contingent" section of the Talent Sheet separately reports on the number of people engaged in the business in the form of 1) part-timers, 2) temporary employees, 3) contractors, 4) consultants, and 5) outsourced labor. The Talent Sheet also shows percentages of these five categories against the total number of full-time employees. This percentage shows management the "mix" of contingent workers used compared to full-time workers, and how close the organization is getting to the fifty-fifty "workforce equilibrium point" wherein the number of full-time employees equals the number of contingent workers.

Since the full-time workforce category is comprised of 1) executives, 2) managers, 3) professionals, and 4) associates, there are some correlations that can be drawn between these two parts of the workforce. For example, when executives/managers don't have the skills or time to look into a certain issue, consultants can be brought in to supplement the existing management team. The same holds true when professionals are not in a large enough "supply." Independent contractors can be brought in to rebalance the professional workload. Finally, when associates in manufacturing, retail, or healthcare are presented with a spike in workload, the temporaries, part-timers, or outsourced workers can be brought in to re-optimize the flow of the human capital supply chain.

Non-workers

Even though the Talent Sheet brings specific attention to the major categories of the full-time and contingent workforces, there is still a third group—"non-workers." This is an unusual group because it represents some of the most experienced talent the organization has available, but they are often ignored in terms of optimizing the human capital supply chain. This group includes those employees who are 1) on leave, 2) retired, 3) on Cobra (recently laid off), and

4) on strike. They are not as easily accessible or available as full-time and contingent workers, but they are still an important part of the supply chain. Even though these workers are often thought of as "off the radar" or "mothballed" like an aircraft carrier, their experience and skills are well known and valuable because they are still relevant in certain situations. Some may argue that this group is worthless and should not be tracked, reported, or taken into consideration in workforce planning activities, but this group may be critical to workforce optimization at both a company and country level. A barrier is that most organizations don't track who these workers are, or where to find them when needed.

Employees on leave or furlough are those full-time employees who are not currently available for full-time work due to such events as maternity or paternity leave, bereavement leave, disability situations, parental care needs, or natural disasters where the employee initiates the decision to take some time off. In the case of furloughs, the worker takes a certain amount of time off (without pay) with a specific back-to-work date. This situation is popular with government agencies in budget trouble or when manufacturing facilities temporarily shut down production. Typical furlough periods can last weeks or even months as the organization tries to correct the situation and bring back their workers. Most workers would rather be furloughed than terminated, because they know up front that they will have their job back at some point. From a Talent Sheet point of view, these workers represent a pool of known talent, and in many cases, are still a cost for the organization.

The next non-worker category on the Talent Sheet represents the organization's already-retired workforce. Organizations that track and update the size, skills, and locations of these retirees are able to quickly tap into this human capital resource pool when it is relevant. Unfortunately, once an employee retires, most organizations remove them from the HR system of record and their work files are put into storage. Since most companies no longer offer corporate pension plans, the need to continually track this talent disappears.

Even though the government may have a record of a worker's contact information, the corporation typically loses track of the retiree over time. Requiring that all retirees are included on the Talent Sheet forces organizations to maintain contact with this talent (within reason) until the retiree dies. There are limitations of course due to ill health or permanent disability, but there are some who are able to be good workers into old age. Some organizations might complain that this tracking requires too much effort and time, but the benefits this worker group represent as potential contingent workers in specific skill sets far outweighs these additional efforts for many organizations.

With the help of social media, the global Internet, and government databases, it is easier to stay in touch with an organization's retiree population and report their numbers on the Talent Sheet. This can be done in the same way that colleges and universities track alumni for the purpose of soliciting donor contributions. Academic institutions are so good at this that a colleague of mine is still receiving fundraising literature sent to her mother who died two years ago at age one hundred. The college has been informed twice of this graduate's death, but perhaps it's easier to keep her in the tracking system. I applaud that kind of the long-term tracking capability, however, deceased people are unlikely to reenter the job market.

Another category of highly skilled but non-working talent includes those employees who have been laid off within the last eighteen months. In the United States, the affected employees can stay on the organization's health insurance plan for a maximum of eighteen months. During that time, the employee will likely look for work, collect unemployment, and stress out over their situation. Unfortunately, many companies cut their ties with these workers and lose contact with them. With the swings in the global employment market, it is not uncommon for companies to hire back these past employees when revenues increase and their skills are needed once again. The organization can track and report upon these workers on the Talent Sheet as a way to maintain awareness about this group of skilled workers. Employees terminated for poor performance and attendance problems are of course flagged.

In addition to laid-off and terminated employees, any employees "on strike" (non-productive) but likely to return are included as the fourth non-worker category. Across Europe, the Middle East, and the United States, it is not uncommon to have large numbers of employees on strike at any point in time. The unavailability of these workers to deliver revenue and drive production can have significant effects on the flow of human capital through the human capital supply chain. If executives, investors, and stockholders know how many employees are on strike at any given time, that information serves as an early warning system that revenues and profits produced by those workers will fall. The Talent Sheet reporting of these individuals brings attention to their numbers, and regular human capital reporting provides focus on the quick resolution of these strikes so that the human capital supply chain can get back in balance.

The three groups of Talent Sheet workers, 1) full-time, 2) contingent and 3) non-workers, are the components of an organization's human capital supply chain—to be tracked, communicated with, and quickly mobilized when needed. This ongoing process of analyzing the requirements of the human capital supply chain and making adjustments to match the needs of the organization with the availability of these pools of talent is the most effective the more often it is reviewed. These workers are the primary "assets" of the organization to be nurtured in order to drive revenues, production, innovation, and customer satisfaction—the prominent features in a successful organization, university, corporation, or government.

> **This ongoing process of analyzing the requirements of the human capital supply chain and making adjustments to match the needs of the organization with the availability of these pools of talent is the most effective the more often it is reviewed.**

To establish and implement the full potential of an optimized human capital supply chain, organizations that are accustomed to annual reviews first initiate quarterly reviews, but ultimately the goal is to make human capital supply chain reviews a weekly process. Like brushing your teeth or regular physical exercise, the long-term rewards will be obvious.

Human Capital Risk on the Talent Sheet

Human capital risks associated with the human capital supply chain workers are also included on the Talent Sheet. Traditional GAAP balance sheets bring attention and disclosure to financial risks the organization is obligated to pay, but many human capital risks are often ignored. The primary human capital risks reported on the Talent Sheet include 1) unfunded pensions/401(k) programs, 2) unpaid payroll, taxes, and insurance, 3) unrecorded vacation/time-off liabilities, 4) potential government fines, and 5) potential employee lawsuit settlements. In many cases, the traditional GAAP or IFRS reporting standards require disclosure only when the "liability" is certain and specific. As an example, Google disclosed in a single line buried in their May 2011 quarterly filing that they have "set aside $500 million for the potential settlement of a Department of Justice investigation into its advertising practices with certain advertisers." By disclosing risks as soon as they become known and reporting their maximum potential cost, investors and stockholders are better able to prepare for the potential impact the risk could have on the organization.

The most volatile of these risks relates to unfunded and underfunded pension plans or 401(k) match programs that are not fully disclosed at the front of an organization's annual report or 10-K. Human capital risks are placed squarely on the Talent Sheet to reveal their magnitude or potential impact on the organization and to flag problems. Corporate CEOs, lawmakers, and many governments faced with huge shortfalls in employee and taxpayer pension funds turn to a strategy that many private companies adopted years ago: moving workers away from guaranteed pension plans and toward self-funded 401(k)-type retirement savings plans.[56] Governors in Ohio and Wisconsin addressed their severe budget problems in the form of contentious showdowns with public employee unions in early 2011 with regard to pensions, wages, and collective bargaining rights. New pension plans are limited and the plans' risk is shifted more to the worker. Some workers prefer a 401(k)-type system because it allows them more control over their retirement assets, including the ability to take the money with them when they change jobs, which occurs more frequently in a knowledge economy.

States that have approved at least a partial changeover from pension plans to 401(k)-type plans (and similar hybrid plans) include Utah, Alaska, Colorado, Georgia, Michigan, and Ohio. As of 2011, states still discussing or considering a similar switch are Kentucky, Oklahoma, Kansas, Florida, North Dakota, Oklahoma, and Virginia. The savings to the states is in the millions each year as new workers are hired. A few states that are not embracing this trend are some with the biggest pension problems: Illinois, California, and New Jersey. Such a switch would not solve their immense shortfalls. Switching workers to 401(k)-type plans can in some cases make the underfunding problem even worse. Most governments, unlike private companies, are constitutionally or contractually prevented from changing the pension plans of current employees without their consent, meaning that the new rules usually apply only to new employees. As more pension contributions from newly hired workers go into individual investment accounts, less money is going into the traditional plan to help finance pensions promised to those older workers. The ability to see these types of workforce-related liabilities is a critical piece of the Talent Sheet's risks section.

Another often unreported human capital risk relates to unpaid payroll taxes and human capital program insurances. Even though

---

56 Steven Greenhouse, "Pension Funds Strained, States Look at 401(k) Plans" *New York Times, Business Day* http://www.nytimes.com/2011/03/01/business/01pension.html?_r=3 &pagewanted=1&seid=auto&smid=tw-nytimespolitics (accessed March 2011).

a company deducts taxes or insurance premiums from a worker's paycheck, the worker is still personally liable for those payments if for some reason the company does not pass those funds to the proper government agency or insurance provider. Organizations can separate the normal quarterly lag in paying many tax and insurance payments from any monies that are over ninety days old. These past-due payments are usually smushed together with the normal ninety-day lag in payments. Any payroll tax or human capital insurance beyond ninety days is listed so that it is clearly seen as a major risk to the employee base. It is a common practice during an organization's bankruptcy for those funds to be spent, which leaves the employees high and dry in debt to the government for unpaid taxes. So, these past-due payments are separately recorded as a "human capital risk" on the Talent Sheet.

Another human capital risk relates to any past due payment to firms that provide temporary, contract, consulting, or outsourced workers to an organization. Any invoice balances not paid within sixty days are reported on the Talent Sheet. The reason this represents a risk is that the staffing firm is paying the contingent worker one week after they perform the service, but the corporation may not pay the staffing firm for thirty to sixty days. The longer these payments are delayed, the longer the staffing firm is left in a tight cash position, jeopardizing the optimized flow of the organization's human capital supply chain.

The third human capital risk relates to the recognition of earned vacation or PTO (personal time off) owed to the employee at some point in the future. These earned hours are typically tracked in the organization HR system of record, but they are usually not monetized or listed as a liability anywhere. This hidden liability will have to be paid at the time an employee is laid off or terminated. During the huge workforce reductions of 2009, many companies were caught off guard by the large amounts of earned vacation they were required by law to pay to laid-off full-time and part-time workers. How much an organization owes in this area is counted as an owed liability. Under

GAAP and IFRS, this type of liability is not required to be consistently reported on the traditional balance sheet. Organizations can choose to report it or ignore it until the time the employee is actually paid the accrued vacation/PTO. But there is no incentive to report these amounts because with GAAP and IFRS, the amount must be reported as a "cost," which would make the report reflect a decrease in profits. That is one way corporations often manipulate P&Ls. Therefore, reporting these different types of human capital risks brings clear attention to any issue that could affect the optimal operation of the human capital supply chain.

A controversial area that is required to be reported in the risk section of the Talent Sheet relates to "potential" government workforce fines. These can be caused by EEOC (equal employment opportunity commission) discrimination findings or wage and hour abuses. Federal or state fines can also be issued for worker compensation or unemployment insurance violations. Since corporations usually do not report the magnitude of these fines until after all appeals have been filed and lost, these amounts have the potential for harm. In a 2011 case, the State of California felt that the Mainstay staffing organization (owned by Native-American tribe) owed the state over $16.4 million in worker compensation payments.[57] Being owned by a Native-American reservation, the staffing firm had operated under what it felt was a legal self-insurance plan. The State of California filed a lien against the staffing firm, froze all their bank accounts, and forced the staffing firm to miss its payroll to about eight thousand temporary workers. This was a huge disruption to many corporate human capital supply chains across the country, but the "potential" liability was never listed anywhere on the staffing firm's GAAP balance sheet, because the issue was still in dispute. Pending fines are often a hidden potential workforce risk that investors and stockholders need to be aware of in order to make well-informed investment decisions about a company or organization.

---

57   Gretchen Gregory, "Mainstay Staffing vs. Employment Development Department," *Staffing Talk*, April 26, 2011 (accessed April 2011) http://staffingtalk.com/mainstay-staffing-employment-development-department/.

The last human capital risk listed on the Talent Sheet is similar in nature to unreported government fines, but it deals with unreported "potential" workforce lawsuits. As with workforce fines, most organizations do not disclose the potential magnitude of any workforce-related lawsuit until the lawsuit is finalized and a settlement amount is known. Since these lawsuits, trials, or negotiations can take years to finalize, no one knows the potential risk the lawsuit poses to the organization. Again, GAAP and IFRS don't require full disclosure until a settlement is reached and, in the meantime, investors are left in the dark about these potential huge liabilities. The "full transparency" nature of the Talent Sheet requires the full potential value of the lawsuit to be listed and adjusted as the negotiations and court case proceeds. When the suit is finalized and payments are made, the organization then reports those final costs on the R&E statement. This level of risk reporting enables investors and shareholders to know whether the organization has enough cash reserves to cover the maximum potential settlement.

As global economies move from a purely financial reporting methodology to a human capital reporting structure, disclosures regarding full-time, contingent, and non-worker groups will make it possible for an organization to keep their human capital supply chain in balance. The information presented between the R&E report and the Talent Sheet brings new focus (for organizations of any size) on the interrelationship between 1) the revenues generated by the workforce, 2) the wage and program costs invested in the workforce, 3) the optimized mix of that workforce, and 4) the risks that could derail the efficient operation of the organization's human capital supply chain. All four reports stand alone and can be reviewed and used independently, but together they form a core reporting structure that provides a clearer picture of a company's financial health in human capital terms.

9 Cash Flow: How to Get from Here to There

HCFR 3 HUMAN CAPITAL TALENT FLOW

	Prior Period	Additions	Voluntary Retirement	Involuntary Termination	As of 12/31/XX	Unfilled Positions
HUMAN CAPITAL TALENT (ASSETS)							
Full-time Executives	#	#	#	#	#	#
Full-time Managers	#	#	#	#	#	#
Full-time Professionals	#	#	#	#	#	#
Full-time Associates/ Manufacturing	#	#	#	#	#	#
Subtotal Fulltime	#	#	#	#	#	#
Part-time Employees	#	#	#	#	#	#
Temporaries	#	#	#	#	#	#
Contractors (1099)	#	#	#	#	#	#
Consultants	#	#	#	#	#	#
Outsourced Labor	#	#	#	#	#	#
Subtotal Contingents	#	#	#	#	#	#
Employees on Leave/Furlough	#	#	#	#	#	
Employees Retired	#	#	#	#	#	
Employees on Cobra	#	#	#	#	#	
Employees on Strike	#	#	#	#	#	
Subtotal Non-working	#	#	#	#	#	
Total Talent Flow	#	#	#	#	#	#
Prior Number of Unfilled Positions	#				#	

THE PREVIOUS CHAPTERS DESCRIBED HOW THE R&E report brings new attention to the creation of "revenues" and the Talent Sheet brings attention to the "workforce mix." These two reports also help us identify two new leading-edge human capital metrics. For the R&E report, the new human capital metric of "revenue per worker" is similar to the old financial ratio of revenue per employee, but now all contingent workers are included in the equation.

For the Talent Sheet, the new human capital metric of "workforce mix" compares the number of full-time employees with the number of contingent workers throughout the organization. The workforce mix metrics help track how close an organization is to the equilibrium point of a fifty-fifty mix of full-time and contingent workers. More detailed information about these human capital metrics and others is included in Chapter 10.

This chapter explores the reasons and format of the different streams of talent flowing through an organization. In any human capital supply chain environment (or manufacturing supply chain environment for that matter), experts agree that the goals are to 1) optimize the flow, 2) reduce costs, and 3) improve quality. The Talent Flow report is similar to its sister report—the Cash Flow statement. Both reports focus on a scarce resource and explain how the availability of that scarce resource changes over a period of time. During the evolution from an industry-based economy to a knowledge-based economy, human capital has replaced financial capital as the driving force behind organizational growth and corporate success. The old mantra of "cash is king" has been replaced with "talent is king and cash is queen."

> **Human capital has replaced financial capital as the driving force behind organizational growth and corporate success.**

Talent Flow Classifications

In the previous chapter, the primary groupings of the global workforce "mix" (full-time, contingent, non-working) and the four to five categories under each of these major groupings were separated to demonstrate their significant impact on an organization's ability to generate revenues and control costs. The headcounts from that prior Talent Sheet are the starting point for the first column of the Talent Flow report. The prior period could be 12/31 of the previous year, last quarter, or last month, depending upon the reporting needs of the organization. From an annual report point of view, the prior period would be last year—and from an SEC point of view, it would be last quarter. Regardless of the time period, the Talent Flow report is focused on explaining changes in the organizations related to 1) workforce mix, 2) change rate, and 3) unfilled positions.

The "workforce mix" is illustrated for both the prior period and the current period, but also explains what changes took place over that time period to create either an increase or decrease in the global workforce. In the traditional financial Cash Flow statement, changes to different cash-related general ledger accounts are classified as either cash balance changes or accrual balance changes. With the new Talent Flow report, changes typically take place because of the hiring/contracting of new workers or the termination of workers. The "change rate" is created by the number of workers 1) added to the workforce, 2) retired, or 3) terminated from the organizations global workforce.

The flow of workers in and out of an "unstable" organization can change rapidly, with large numbers leaving and a large number being hired, but without this Talent Flow tracking, everything seems stable to the investor or stockholder. This hidden instability of a "revolving-door workforce" hurts the generation of revenues as unskilled or inexperienced workers try to replace existing employees for a multitude of reasons, such as a poor work environment or terrible management. The Talent Flow report brings attention to this potential problem, but it also brings attention to specific problem categories, illustrating the number of unfilled positions by worker category and percentage of unfilled positions compared to the total workforce population. Organizations, along with their executives, stockholders, and taxpayers are able to see how these numbers play out. Example: If an organization has high levels of unfilled positions in their executive or professional ranks (especially sales), this can have a direct impact on the generation of revenues in the short term and on the organization's ability to achieve its goals. Overall, the workforce mix, the change rate, and the unfilled position information derived from the Talent Flow report can be an eye-opener for everyone involved when it is included in the annual report or 10-K filings.

The top of the Talent Flow report has six columns. The first column labeled "Prior Period" comes directly from a prior Talent Sheet listing of human capital asset categories separated between 1) full-time, 2) contingent, and 3) non-working. This is the starting point in the Talent Flow report. The next column, "Additions," represents all workers who have been added to your organization during the reporting period. This includes all full-time new hires and any additional contingent workers who have been added to the organization's workforce. The next two columns of "Voluntary Retirements" and "Involuntary Terminations" address any reductions in that workforce. These two columns are separated in order show which workers left of their own choice and which workers were terminated, laid off, or fired.

The fifth column records the "total as-of date" column that adds the prior period plus additions, minus retirements, minus terminations, equals Total Workforce. This total column shows how many total workers are currently involved in the global organization, and ties back to the Talent Sheet totals. This is also the column that makes it possible to calculate a new mix ratio of contingent workers compared to full-time employees. The sixth column of "Unfilled Positions" gives the stakeholders an idea of how many more workers the organization needs to achieve its current strategic and financial goals.

The goal of all of these Talent Flow report columns is to provide critical information about the types of workers that are "flowing" through your organization as well as how they are entering and leaving your workforce. This is valuable information to C-level leaders and their boards of directors who can apply the concepts of supply chain optimization to this flow to increase an organization's productivity and profitability.

10 Financial Ratios: Looking at HR Metrics and HR Analytics

HCFR 4 HUMAN CAPITAL METRICS

	Prior Period	Current Period	+/−
REVENUE & EXPENSE METRICS: (TOP 5)			
Revenue $ Per Full-time Employee	$	$	$
Total Wage Expense to Revenue	%	%	%
Total HC Program Expense to Revenue	%	%	%
Total Non-HC Expenses to Revenue	%	%	%
Revenue $ Per Worker (all 5 categories)	$	$	$
TALENT SHEET METRICS: (TOP 5)			
% Mix of Contingents to Total Workforce	%	%	%
% Mix of Non-workers to Total Workforce	%	%	%
% Mix of Full-timers to Total Workforce	%	%	%
% Total Workforce Change	%	%	%
% of Total Workforce Change to Revenue Change	%	%	%
HC TALENT FLOW METRICS: (TOP 5)			
% of Position Changes to Total Workforce	%	%	%
% of Full-time Position Changes	%	%	%
% of Open Positions to Full-time	%	%	%
% of Contingent Position Changes	%	%	%
% of Non-working Position Changes	%	%	%

ONE OF THE RULES OF TRADITIONAL FINANCIAL RATIO analysis from my accounting classes back in the 1980s at Duquesne University in Pittsburgh, Pennsylvania, was that financial ratios need to originate from the data provided on one of the three core financial statements (P&L, balance sheet, or cash flow). You cannot bring in "outside data" because the reader of any annual report or 10-K would not have access to that same source data. The same principle holds true for human capital metrics, where **ratio percentages** or **dollar amounts** must originate from one of the three core human capital financial reports (R&E, talent sheet, or talent flow). Because of this rule, some financial statements (especially the balance sheets) have expanded over the years, with additional pages of "disclosures" in order to include the information needed to calculate more complicated financial ratios.

Of the four human capital financial reports, this one is probably the **least standard**. There are hundreds of different HR metrics currently in use across the thousands of companies around the globe. The current efforts (by the Society for Human Resource Management, the American National Standards Institute, and the International Standards Organization) to create a set of global HR standardized metrics is evidence of the desperate need among investors, stockholders, and executives to better understand their workforce and its strong connection to the success of their organization. One of the first HR metrics working its way through the standardization process with SHRM, ANSI, and ISO relates to the cost-per-hire standard. Oddly, this type of metric is of more interest to HR professionals than it is to the investment community. This forty-three-page standard describes the proper way to calculate all the costs related to hiring a full-time employee. Even though this metric does not draw all of its components from the three human capital financial reports, it is a valuable first step in the movement toward global standards.

Within the human capital metrics report, the focus is on those fifteen metrics that have the most direct relationships between the workforce and organizational success. All of the hundreds of HR metrics have some relationship to revenues, profits, and productivity, but human capital financial report metrics have the strongest correlations to 1) revenue generation, 2) workforce mix, and 3) human capital supply chain flow optimization.

Revenue and Expense Metrics

The generation of revenues is directly related to the productivity of the workforce. Enhanced productivity has benefits to corporations as well as entire countries, as workers achieve higher levels of output. This can be in the form of more sales per salesperson, more unit output per factory worker, more resolutions per support person, or more patents per engineer. It all relates back to "output" per worker.

The first two HCFR metrics are 1) revenue per full-time employee and 2) revenue per worker. The revenue per full-time employee has been around for fifty years and is one of the few human capital metrics that most C-level executives, investors, and taxpayers have used with confidence and is valuable in comparing revenue per full-time employee across different companies and different industries. Unfortunately, the revenue per full-time employee has become less and less relevant as organizations use more and more contingent workers in all aspects of their operation. For that reason, the "revenues per global worker" (combining full-time and contingent workers) is a far more accurate measure of the number of workers it takes to generate revenues and to drive the organization forward.

The next three Revenue & Expense metrics refer to those "investments" in the workforce that enable it to generate revenues, products, and happy customers. An analysis of total wages paid to all workers compared to the amount of revenue generated demonstrates the relationship between base wage, commission, and bonus payments to the productivity and output of the entire workforce. Studies have shown that compensation is not the main motivator for most workers, but it is high on the list and usually represents the single highest cost to the organization.

Increasing wage costs each year is not a problem as long as revenues grow at a faster pace. The investment in wages usually signifies a net increase in the number of workers required by the organization to generate those revenues and activities. For all these reasons, the human capital metrics report also includes 1) wage expense to revenue percentage, 2) human capital program expense to revenue percentage, and 3) non-human-capital expense to revenue percentage. The amounts and rates of investments in these wages, programs, and non-human-capital expenses have the most direct impact on productivity and output.

Talent Sheet Metrics

This set of five human capital metrics brings attention to the mix and structure of an optimized workforce. As organizations move toward a fifty-fifty workforce equilibrium between full-time and contingent workers, and by comparing these Talent Sheet metrics over time with the R&E metrics, it is possible to see how quickly, and whether, a more "flexible" workforce actually improved the productivity, revenue, and success of an organization—or whether further mix adjustments are needed. A similar correlation exists between the flexibility of a nation's workforce and its increased generation of output in the form of GDP (gross domestic product). In both cases, enhanced flexibility leads to greater productivity, which leads to increasing output/revenue.

> **Enhanced flexibility leads to greater productivity, which leads to increasing output/revenue.**

The first Talent Sheet "mix" metric looks at the percentage mix of contingent workers to the total workforce. Those who argue that they only need to compare contingent workers to full-time employees are neglecting to include the costs of the non-workers within the overall

Financial Ratios: Looking at HR Metrics and HR Analytics

human capital supply chain. As with all of these metrics, looking at the "change in the percentages" over time makes it possible to evaluate whether the organization's workforce performance is getting better or worse. (Also look at the percentage mix of non-workers to the total workforce as well as the percentage mix of full-timers to the total workforce.) By monitoring these ever-changing percentages over time, an organization can actually observe their transition from an industrial-based "lifer" workforce to a knowledge-based "flexible" workforce.

The total workforce change percentage gives investors an overall understanding of how fast the organization's workforce is growing or shrinking and the correlation to growth or decline in workforce costs. For example, an organization may have a stable workforce number, but costs are dropping because of the use of more part-time or temporary employees.

The total workforce change to revenue change percentage illustrates how the workforce is growing or shrinking in relation to revenue changes. By monitoring this percentage on a regular basis, imbalances are quickly evident between workforce size and revenue. If this type of metric had been watched more carefully in 2008, organizations could have adjusted their workforce size and mix over time, rather than having to lay off seven million people in the United States over such a short time span.

If local, state, and federal government agencies had monitored and managed this relationship between workforce size and tax revenue, a slower reduction in the government workforce could have begun as soon as tax revenues started to decline in 2008. Because lawmakers at all levels of US and foreign governments sat on their hands until 2011 to address this obvious imbalance between workforce size and tax revenues, many government bodies are now looking at massive 15- to 25-percent workforce reductions to "balance their budgets." A simple human capital metric coupled with proactive management action could have once again averted massive workforce reductions and the unintended consequences they created.

The metrics section of the Talent Flow report shows the percentage of position changes to the total workforce. This metric is a good indicator of the flow rate moving through the human capital supply chain because it totals up all of the inflows and outflows of talent through the organization. Because all "flows" are considered, an investor can determine how much "churn" there is in any organization. An organization with a lot of churn is usually more unstable than an organization with less churn, depending upon the industry. Consider that if an organization has 30- to 50-percent worker turnover, that means extra training, orientation, and learning curves must be initiated.

The second metric relates to the percentage of full-time position changes, where the churn principle is narrowed to the flow of talent in and out of just the full-time talent pool, compared to the total full-time headcount. Remember that in all of these calculations, we do NOT refer to full-time equivalents (FTEs) because we want to know the numbers of bodies (i.e., unique skill sets) in use throughout the organizations. Smushing talent together into FTEs distorts the amount of talent actually needed to optimize the human capital supply chain. While many organizations' full-time employees still make up the largest part of their workforce, this metric brings attention to the actual stability of this talent pool.

For many organizations, there are always open full-time positions that hold the company back from achieving maximized revenue. Those organizations that have an efficient recruiting department or RPO (recruitment process outsourcing) partner have the best chance of keeping this percentage as low as possible. There will always be a need to find new talent in any organization, especially as the seventy-eight million US baby boomers retire, but those operations that can minimize those open positions while still maintaining the quality of new workers have the best chance for optimizing their success. There are many other HR metrics such as time-to-hire, cost-per-hire, and quality-per hire, which are very important to the management of any recruitment operation, but they are not directly tied to the information illustrated in the three core human capital financial reports.

To identify the "rate of flow" through any human capital supply chain and the resulting churn of talent it can create for the organization, we need to know the percentage of contingent position changes as well as the percentage of non-working position changes. These metrics help to explain how fast these two separate flows of talent move through the organization. For example, if a company is adding more contingent workers than they are eliminating, they are moving toward a more flexible workforce. In the same light, if an organization's non-working population numbers are exploding due to retirements and strikes, the organization may need to be prepared to back-fill that lost talent. In both metrics, the flow within these workforce categories and their active management are critical to the eventual mix- and flow-rate optimization of the human capital supply chain.

Every organization is different, but the use of these human capital metrics provides performance comparisons across companies, industries, and even countries. Being able to open up any annual report or 10-K document and understand the human capital strengths of an organization is just as important as knowing their EBITDA (earnings before interest, taxes, depreciation, and accruals) or stock price. These fifteen core HCSC metrics are the start to fine-tuning and optimizing any human capital supply chain. They analyze the information provided on the three core reports in a way that transforms data into actionable information.

> **Being able to open up any annual report or 10-K document and understand the human capital strengths of an organization is just as important as knowing their EBITDA (earnings before interest, taxes, depreciation, and accruals) or stock price.**

There are many ways to track the effectiveness of any workforce, such as the future-oriented analytics conducted at Minneapolis-based weapons-maker, Alliant Techsystems, Inc. (ATK). ATK hired statisticians in their armaments unit to develop a workforce planning system, which has been highly effective in identifying and dealing with talent management challenges. Their "flight risk" model divided the company by department and by individual to identify who exactly represented the biggest risk of leaving the company. A defense company like ATK does not have a lot of people working in the same positions, doing the same things. They more likely have one highly specialized person who is an expert in some area without a lot of overlap in job duties. That means there is a greater potential for negative consequences and disruption in their work if an expert leaves the company. Such companies must pay close attention and plan for potential changes. For example, in a situation of national security, an analysis of the possible consequences must be made from many angles.

In one ATK operation, the main threat was the potential departure of an engineer who was "central to a major initiative of the armaments unit."[58] According to the analytics, his age and tenure with the company were both "flight-risk factors." Armed with this knowledge, the company could then prepare for the worker's possible departure in any number of ways, i.e., assigning an apprentice to learn from the engineer, etc. This use of sophisticated data analysis and modeling has put ATK at the forefront in the use of human capital metrics and analytics to predict workforce needs.

Any human capital metric must be 1) easy to calculate, 2) simple to explain, and 3) actionable. This is not as easy as it sounds, since most organizations in 2011 still use antiquated HRIS systems that are often not even integrated between departments or divisions. New SaaS-based human capital management solutions such as Workday.com and BondTalent-US.com are examples of web 2.0 solutions that bring all the information concerning your full-time, contingent, and non-worker workforce together into a cloud-based software envi-

---

58 Ed Frauenheim, "Personnel Precision: To stay on target in its workforce planning, weapons-maker ATK uses sophisticated metrics analysis to anticipate flight risks and the need for reinforcements." *Workforce Management*, March 1, 2011 http://www.highbeam.com/doc/1G1-251107607.html (accessed March 2011).

ronment using a single database for the entire organization. A key challenge is getting an entire organization on board with the same single-database solution. The metrics are intended to help any organization better understand and evaluate their entire workforce in relation to 1) maximized revenue, 2) most productive workforce mix, and 3) optimized flow rates.

11 C-levels, Investors, Government, and Citizens Call to Action: An Open Letter

DEAR CEOs, CFOs, COOs, CHROs, INVESTMENT community, vendors, government, workforce members, human resources, and the staffing industry:

In 2011, Jeffrey A. Joerres, Manpower Inc. chairman, president, and CEO, introduced the notion that a new era is upon us—the Human Age, wherein optimized human potential is the single most important determinant of business growth and success. Business and government leaders will need to reexamine how they unleash and leverage human potential in an environment that is increasingly volatile and constantly shifting. The nature of this environment will need workers who have the required "specific skills, behaviors, and ways of operating" in a "chaotic global environment."

Talent and human potential will replace financial capital as the dominant resource, the catalyst for change, and the global driving force economically, politically, and socially. Joerres contends that technology has become "the great leveler, allowing skilled individuals to vault the restrictions of national borders and migration caps, as it has liberated the talented individual to undertake professional jobs anywhere in the world, and dictate how, when, and where they work."[59]

---

59 Jeffrey A. Joerres, "Entering the Human Age: Thought Leadership Insights." Introduction to Manpower Inc. Papers 2011.

I have admitted in these pages that I have an interest in a "revolution" of sorts in the way the world does business and in the role of our country in the global economy. You and I have an important stake in making business more efficient. The worker in Tunisia made a big statement by setting himself on fire. His singular action forced the world to pay attention to the economic and social situation in his country and region. The concepts in *Human Capital Financial Reports* (and the rest of the series) reflect my intent to fan a fire of sorts in the minds of Americans.

I am not comfortable watching America drift into the back of the pack in our business dealings, finance, and industry. And I don't think most Americans have any idea what it will mean to become just another developed country. What's so bad about that? Well, when you fall back in the pack, you risk becoming mediocre—standards of living deteriorate beneath us. Many Americans have already experienced this feeling firsthand with the slipping away of the security of home ownership. Owning a home doesn't offer the sure promise of growing equity anymore for many Americans. Sixty percent of mortgages are underwater—meaning that the owners owe more on the home than the home is worth. Widespread rental arrangements are far more common in other developed countries that are not used to the prosperity that most Americans have taken for granted over the last fifty years. Americans fully expect our first responders (police, fire, ambulance, medical personnel) to be fast, efficient, and reliable. My friend in Europe watched his cab driver have a heart attack and die in the twenty-five minutes it took the ambulance to arrive. Firefighter response is slower and medical response is even slower in most other countries. We like to believe that the United States is better than that—how many Americans will stand for the reduction in quality and efficiency that will surely occur if we don't address our workforce issues? Complacency cannot be tolerated. Our goal must be to increase productivity, reduce costs, and improve quality.

> **To maintain the prosperity that we often take for granted, we have to be more productive. To be more productive, we have to be more efficient. To be more efficient, we have to optimize our workforce.**

The United States has a history of being strong on productivity. And we, as Americans, are used to thinking of ourselves as the best. But, to maintain the prosperity that we often take for granted, we have to be more productive. To be more productive, we have to be more efficient. To be more efficient, we have to optimize our workforce. By optimizing our workforce, the result will be higher productivity. If we don't do these things, other countries will. And those countries will move forward, and the United States will continue to slide backward and lose the global prosperity we have become so accustomed to.

We cannot rely on someone else to solve the inevitable workforce dilemmas we face with 40 percent fewer workers available over the coming years as baby boomers retire. We will have to run our businesses, our government, and our economy and meet all the needs with little more than half the workers. Technology is one factor that will continue to offer solutions but technology is not enough. We must propel and optimize our workforce if we hope to sustain the lifestyles and economic successes we have enjoyed for so long. Essential changes are needed on a large scale in every business, organization, and government to be more efficient. The right people have to have the right information at the right time in order to optimize the human capital supply chain.

Optimization of the human capital supply chain creates more operational efficiency, and coupling that with the human capital financial reporting tools gives us the mechanisms to measure and improve how well we are doing and protect us from the easily manipulated and misleading reporting methods that put the US and the rest of the world in the vulnerable financial position we find ourselves in. The time is now to focus on the workforce—which creates the revenues and drives the success of any organization.

Yours sincerely,
Tim Giehll

Your feedback is welcome! Contact Tim Giehll.
Tim.Giehll@BondTalent-US.com
Cell: 715-828-0873
www.HumanCapitalFinancialReports.com

Acknowledgments

I AM GRATEFUL TO THOSE PEOPLE THAT HELPED ME develop my thoughts around the first book in this trilogy, *Human Capital Supply Chains*: my thanks to the late Dr. Edward Deming (Global Thought Leader) for his breakthrough work in World Class Manufacturing Techniques, Jack Welch (former CEO at General Electric) for his global support for Six Sigma principles, and Mike Stankey (president of WorkDay software) for believing in my ideas and sharing them with his entire company.

As these ideas naturally led to *Human Capital Financial Reports*, I thank Dr. Jac Fitz-enz (CEO at Human Capital Source) and Jeff Higgins (CEO at HCMI) for our shared long-standing beliefs in the principles of HR reporting metrics and for encouraging me to take my ideas one step further.

Finally, thanks to writer Marly Cornell for her insightful collaboration with this project and in helping to put these concepts in an accessible format. As always, thanks to my wife and wonderful family.

About the Author

TIM GIEHLL IS A STAFFING INDUSTRY VETERAN, technology visionary, and manufacturing expert of more than thirty years. He has served since 1999 as US CEO of Bond Talent & Bond eEmpACT software (a Bond International Software Company), where he has worked with hundreds of temporary staffing firms to automate and optimize their operations.

Giehll developed his understanding of complex software environments during the 1990s as CFO for world-renowned supercomputer designer Steve Chen during their $150-million technology venture with IBM and Sequent Computers. He worked in the 1980s as a manufacturing accounting manager with Control Data. After meeting with industry visionary Edward Deming in the early '80s, he was instrumental in launching Control Data's world-class manufacturing initiatives, especially just-in-time inventory processes.

Giehll serves on the Society of Human Resource Management's (SHRM) Investor Metrics Workgroup which is developing consistent US and global HR Metric standards, which will eventually be required in annual reports and 10-K filings. He is an active member of the American Staffing Association, Staffing Industry Analysts, and Leading Edge HR Networks. Since 2009, he has presented his revolutionary human capital concepts all over the world at conferences and webinars including those organized by The Conference Board, *CFO Magazine*, Staffing Management Chicago, HR.com, HRchitect, *Business Analysts Times*, Thought Leadership Institute, Staffing World, and the Human Capital Institute. *Human Capital Financial Reports* is Giehll's second book.

Index

10-K, xiii, 68
401(k) plans, 90–91

A
Absenteeism, 34
Accenture, 34–35
Accounting Today, 29
Adecco, 11–12
Alliant Techsystems, Inc. (ATK), 107–108
Analytics, 34–36, 52–53, 62
Annual reports, xiii, 68
ANSI (American National Standards Institute), 42–44, 102
AOL (America Online), 28
Arthur Anderson, 22 n.27
ASA (American Staffing Association), 84 n.54
Asia, 22, 84
Assets
  in GAAP, 49
  in HCFR, 58–59
AT&T (American Telephone & Telegraph), 71
Authorities. *See* Regulators and authorities
Automation of financial systems, 18

B
Baby Boomers, 10, 75–76, 83–84, 106, 113
Background checks, 13, 75
Balance sheets, 49–50. *See also* Talent sheets
Balancing the workforce, 12, 86
Bartz, Carol, 73
Bassi, Laurie, xiii–xiv, xv n.4, xvi, 42
Bell Atlantic, 29
Bemis, Jane, xiii, xvi
Bernanke, Ben, 30–31

Big Four auditing firms, 22, 38, 42–45
Board of director incentives, 26, 72
BondTalent-US.com, 108–109
Bonuses, 26, 30, 72–73, 75, 103
Bussey, John, 85 n.55

C
California
  a city near bankruptcy, 59
  pension problems, 90-91
  staffing firm owed workers' comp payments, 93–94
Call to action, 111–114
Canadian credit union, 35–36
Cappelli, Peter, 15
Cash flow, 50–51, 95–99
Caterpillar Inc., 16 n.21
Censky, Annalynn, 30–31 nn.38–39
CEOs (chief executive officers). *See* C-level leaders
Change rate, 97
China, 70, 85
Chrysler, 28
C-level leaders. *See also* Compensation
  call to action, 111–114
  and human resource departments, 35
  recognizing need for HCSC model, 18
Cloud-based software, 108–109
CNN (Cable News Network), 25 n.30, 30 n.38
Co-employment laws, 84–85
Commission costs, 71–72, 103
Company operations, 32–33
Compaq, 28
Compensation
  bonuses, 26, 30, 72–73
  commission, 71–72
  executive, 25–26, 81–82

119

human capital metrics, 103–104
overtime, 70–71
perks, 72–73
The Conference Board, xiii, 47, 119
Consultants, 85. *See also* Contingent workforce
Contingent workforce
advantages of, 3
alternative views, 15–16
benefits of, 12–14
challenges, 16–18
disclosure, 15–16
financial advantages, 16
flexibility, 10–12, 15–16
global spending, 17
growth of, 3, 11–12
number of workers, 17
talent sheet, 83–86
technological changes, 10–12
Contractors, 11, 14, 84–85. *See also* Contingent workforce
Cost of goods sold (COGS)
in GAAP, 48
in HCFR, 57
Cost-per-hire, 75, 104, 106
Credit scores, 15 n.14
Customer relationship management (CRM) systems, 18

D

Daimler, 28
Deloitte Touche Tohmatsu Limited (DTTL), 22, 38
Demming, Edward, 25
Department of Labor, unemployment rate, 3–4
Depression, 7
Disclosures, 29, 90–94, 102
Discouraged workers, 5
Disney, xiii, 41
Dodd-Frank Wall Street Reform and Consumer Protection Act, 30, 31, 39
Drug screenings, 13
Duffield, Dave, 19

E

EBITDA (Earnings before interest, taxes, depreciation, and adjustments), 107
The Economist, 76 n.53
EEOC (Equal Employment Opportunity Commission) violations, 93

Enron, 29
Entering the Human Age, 47
Enterprise resource planning (ERP) systems, 18, 63
Equity
in GAAP, 50
in HCFR, 61
Ernst & Young Global Limited (EYG), 22, 38
Europe, 22, 84, 89, 112
E-Verify, 75
Everyone sells, 71–72
Executives. *See* C-level leaders
Exxon, 29

F

Facebook, 29
FAF (Financial Accounting Foundation), 40
FASAC (Financial Accounting Standards Advisory Council), 41
FASB (Financial Accounting Standards Board), 40–42, 44
Federal Reserve, 30–31
Financial crisis. *See* Great Recession
Financial ratios, 51. *See also* Analytics; Metrics
Financial statements
GAAP compared to human capital financial reports, 24
human capital financial reports, 33–36
manipulating, 24–25
new rules needed, 22–24
regulatory perspective, 29–36
short-term profits danger, 24–27, 27–29
Financial systems, automation of, 18
Fines for regulatory violations, 93–94
Fishman, Jay, 72
Fitz-enz, Jac, xiii, xvi
Flexibility of workforce, 10–12, 15–16, 104–105
Flight risk model, 108
Ford, Henry, 19
Forecasting, 33–34, 52
Fortune, 34 n.40
Frauenheim, Ed, 15 n.20, 16 n.23, 108 n.58
Freelancers. *See* Contingent workforce
FTEs (full-time equivalents), 106
FTSE (London Stock Exchange), 25

Index 121

Full-time workforce, 81–83
Furloughed workers, 87–89

G
GAAP (Generally Accepted Accounting Principles)
  evolution to IFRS, 38–42
  limits of, 21–22
  misleading, 4
  NET profit, 67
  part of global financial reporting method, 44–46
  reasons for change, 47–52
  standard formats, 47–52
GASAC (Governmental Accounting Standards Advisory Council), 41
GASB (Governmental Accounting Standards Board), 41
GDP (gross domestic product), 104
GE (General Electric), 14
Gecko, Gordon, 26 n.33
General and administrative (G&A) expenses
  in GAAP, 48
  in HCFR, 58
Germany, xvi, 45
Girard, Kim, 29 n.37
Gladwell, Malcolm, 6
Global financial reporting, 44–46. *See also* IFRS (international financial reporting standards)
Global knowledge, xvi, 7, 14, 26
Google, 29, 90
Government
  call to action, 111–114
  workforce, 59, 91–94, 105
Great Depression, 7
Great Recession, xii–xiii, 2, 3, 6–7, 9, 12 n.16, 16, 24, 30–31, 68–69, 74
Greenberg, Herb, 28, 28 n.35
Greenhouse, Steven, 91 n.56
Gregory, Gretchen, 93 n.57
Grey's Anatomy, 14
GTE (Gran Tierra Energy, Inc.), 29

H
Healthcare costs, 13, 16, 73–74
Hidden workforce, 2
Higgins, Jeff, xvi, 47
Hilton Hotels and Resorts, 15

HP (Hewitt Packard), 28
HPI (human potential indices), 45, 111
Human Age, 111
Human capital analytics, 34–36, 52–53, 62
Human capital financial reports (HCFRs)
  benefits of, 26–27, 80
  birth of, 47–53
  forward-looking, 33–36
  frequency of reviews, 90
  necessity of, 7
  new analytics, 52–53
  structure of, 55–63
Human Capital Global Management (HCGM), 17 n.26
Human Capital Management Institute, 47
Human capital metrics
  definition and purpose, 62, 63
  proposed formulation and standardization, 43
  relationship to company performance, 42–43
  sample sheet, 101
Human capital program expenses, 57, 70–76
Human capital revenue. *See* Revenue and human capital expense statements (R&E)
Human capital risk, 90–94
Human Capital Source, xiii
Human Capital Supply Chain (HCSC)
  automation, 19
  defined, 1
  department, 32–33
  frequency of reviews, 90
  perfect storm, 18–20
Human capital value added (HCVA), 67, 78
Human capital wage expenses, 56–57, 69–70
Human resources
  automation of transactions, 10
  and goals of the CEO, 34–35
  leaders' role, 10–11
  software, 18–19, 68, 108–109
  traditional and forward-looking, 33
Husz, Martin, 1

I
IBM (International Business Machines), 70

IFRS (international financial reporting standards)
  generally, 22–23
  adoption of, 22 n.28, 38–40
  advantages of, 23, 41–42
  concerns about, 41
  global financial reporting method, 44–46
Independent contractors, 11, 14, 84–85. *See also* Contingent workforce
India, 70
Industry-based economy, xvi, 1–2, 4, 17–18, 21
Insurance, 13, 16, 73–74, 91–92
Internet, 18
Investments in the workforce, 103–104
Investors, 24–28, 49–50, 59–61, 111–114
IPad, 14
IQPC (International Quality & Productivity Center), 35 n.41
Irani, Ray, 72
ISO (International Standards Organization), 42–44, 102

J
Japan, xvi
JIT (just-in-time) production processes, xvi, 18
Joerres, Jeffrey A., 111

K
Kelly Girl, 12
Kmart, 28
Knowledge-based economy, xvi, 1–2, 4, 17–18, 21
KPMG International Cooperative (KPMG), 22, 38

L
Laid off workers, 88–89
Lampert, Eddie, 28
Lawsuits, 94
Lehman Brothers, 6, 30
Liabilities
  in GAAP, 49–50
  in HCFR, 60–61

M
MacDonald, Jim, 15
Mainstay staffing organization, 93
Manpower Inc., 12, 47, 113
McBassi & Co., xiii–xv
MCI, 28
McMurrer, Dan, xiii
Medicare, 13
Mergers, 27–29
Metrics, 42–43, 62, 63, 101, 104–109
Microsoft, 3
Military, 17–18
Missildine-Martin, Cathy, 35 n.41
Mobil, 29
Moore, Rebecca, 12 n.16
MRP (manufacturing resource planning) systems, 18
Mui, Ylan Q., 2
Mulligan, Casey, 15 n.15

N
National Presto Industries, 69
Navy, 17
Net profit, 67, 78
New York Times, 11 n.15, 59 n.50, 91 n.56
Nextel, 28
Non-human-capital expenses, 57–58, 76–77
Nonprofits, 7, 70
Non-workers, 87–89
North Africa, 6

O
OECD (Organization of Economic Cooperation and Development), 76
Ohio, 73, 91–92
On-call workers. *See* Contingent workforce
On-leave workers, 87–89
Optimization, 1, 12, 20, 76, 78, 106, 113
Outsourcing, 70, 85–86
Overtime, 70–71

P
Part-time workforce. *See* Contingent workforce
Payroll taxes, 73, 92
Pennsylvania, 73
Pension liabilities, 76, 91–92
Peoplesoft, 19
Perks, 72, 82. *See also specific perks by name*
Predictive models, 33

Index   123

Prescription drugs, 13, 73–74
PricewaterhouseCoopers International Limited (PwCIL), 22, 29, 38
Productivity, 103, 104, 113
Profit and loss statements (P&L), 48–49. *See also* Revenue and human capital expense statements (R&E)
Program expenses, 70–76
PTO (paid time off), 92

Q
Quaker Oats, 28

R
Rate of flow, 106–107
Recession. *See* Great Recession
Recruitment, 74–75, 106
Regulators and authorities
  Big Four auditing firms, 38, 42–44
  difficulty of change, 45–46
  Financial Accounting Standards Board, 37, 38, 40–42, 44
  global financial reporting method needed, 44–45
  Securities and Exchange Commission, 29, 37, 39–40, 44
  Society for Human Resource Management, 37, 38, 42–45, 47, 102
Relocation costs, 74–75
Research and development (R&D)
  in GAAP, 48
  in HCFR, 57
Retention of workers, 74
Retired workers, 87–88
Retirement savings plans, 90–91
Revenue and expense metrics, 103–104
Revenue and human capital expense statements (R&E), 55–58, 65–78
Revenues per global worker, 103
Risk, 29, 90–94
RPO (recruitment process outsourcing), 106

S
SaaS (Software as a Service), 68, 108–109
Sales and marketing (S&M)
  in GAAP, 48
  in HCFR, 57
Sarbanes-Oxley Act (SOX), 29, 31
Schapiro, Mary, 39

Sears, 28, 33
SEC (Securities and Exchange Commission), 29, 37, 39–40, 44
Self-employment, 14. *See also* Contingent workforce; Contractors
Short-term mentality, 24–27, 27–29, 32
SHRM (Society for Human Resource Management)
  creating global standardized metrics, 102
  global financial reporting method, 44–45
  Investor Metrics Workgroup, 43, 47
  purpose of, 37–38, 42–44
SI Review (Staffing Industry Review), 9 n.13
Sieker, Achim, 45
Signing bonuses, 75
Skype, 14
Snapple, 28
Social unrest, 5
Software, 18–19, 108–109
Spreadsheets, 18
Sprint, 28
Staffing firms
  and human capital analytics, 52–53
  past due payments as risk, 92–93
  services provided, 12–13
Staffing Industry Analysts (SIA), 16 n.22, 17 n.25
Stanger, Allison, xv
Stankey, Mike, 16 n.24
StarTribune, 11 n.14
Stephenson, Randall L., 72
Stewart, Martha, 73
Stock grants and options, 75
Storage Tek, 28
Striking workers, 89
Sun Microsystems, 28
Sutphin, Brian, 28
Symmetry Software, 73 n.52

T
Talent
  defined, 1, 2
  demographics, 26
  as dominant resource, 111
  long term growth, 53
  recruitment, 74–75, 106
  reengaging, 5
  retaining, 9

search, 10
skills matching, 31–32
Talent flow
   classifications, 97–99
   compared to cash flow, 61–62
   goal of, 99
   sample sheet, 95
Talent sheets
   generally, 58–61, 80–81
   contingent workforce, 83–86
   full-time workforce, 81–83
   human capital risk, 90–94
   metrics, 104–109
   sample sheet, 79
Taxpayers, 30, 59–61
Technology, 10–12, 14, 16
Telberg, Rick, 29
Temporary workers, 11. *See also* Contingent workforce
Terminated workers, 88–89
Testing of employees, 13
Time Warner, 28
Time-to-hire, 75, 106
Tipping point, 6
Tobak, Steve, 27 n.34
Towers Watson & Co., 15
Training, 13–14, 74
Transparency, xiii, xvi, 7
Tuition reimbursement, 13–14, 74
Tunisian worker, 6, 112
Twitter, 14

U
UK (United Kingdom), 22, 25
Unemployed workers, 2
Unemployment
   causes of, 30–31
   insurance, 74, 93–94
   rate, 3–4
Unfilled positions, 98
Unions, 83, 91
Unstable organizations, 97–98, 106

V
Vacation earned, 92
VanderMey, Anne, 34 n.40
Variable human inventory. *See* Talent sheets
Verizon, 29
Virtual staff. *See* Contingent workforce

W
Wage expenses, 56–57, 69–70
Wahlquist, Richard, 84 n.54
Wall Street, xvi, 26, 30
Walmart, 20
Washington Post, 24 n.29
Web 2.0, 108–109
Weidner, Justin, 31
Welch, Jack, 14
Weldon, Mary, xii n.1
Wharton School, 15
Williams, John, 31
Wisconsin
   appliance manufacturer, 69
   government pensions, 91
Woodford, Brent, 41
Workday, 19, 108–109
Workers' compensation, 74, 93–94
Workforce
   balance, 12, 86
   flexibility, 10–12, 15–16, 104–105
   inequality, xiv–xv
   investments in, 103–104
   mix, 97–98
   transaction rates, 80
WorldCom, 28, 29

Y
Yang, Jia Lynn, 24 n.29